HealthCare.com
R_X for Reform

HealthCare.com
R_X for Reform

David B. Friend, M.D., MBA

Watson Wyatt Worldwide

S^t_L

St. Lucie Press
Boca Raton   London   New York   Washington, D.C.

Library of Congress Cataloging-in-Publication Data

Friend, David (David B.)
    Healthcare. com: Rx for reform / by David Friend
        p. cm.
    Includes index.
    ISBN 1-57444-274-0 (alk paper)
    1. Medical care--United States. 2. Medical economics--United
States 3. Medical policy--United States. I. Title.
    RA395.A3F7631999
    362.1' 0973--dc21

    for Library of Congress   99-40268
CIP

Preface

Despite having undergone more than a decade of change, the U.S. health care delivery system is still in the early innings of its transformation to a truly effective, cost efficient and compassionate provider of care. Despite the enormous turmoil the health care system has undergone — from the proliferation of managed care to the closing of hospitals — the system is still failing large numbers of people and is arguably becoming progressively sicker. To the author, who has been trained in both business and medicine, at least six major symptoms present themselves:

1. **Health care costs are accelerating**. Profit pressures from shareholders on the managed care industry are driving price increases. The industry is playing catch-up after seeing its profit margins and stock prices shrink due to a costly grab for market share combined with inadequate management and operational control systems.
2. **The quality of patient care is uncertain at best**. The phrase "quality care" borders on being an oxymoron, remaining both undefined and difficult to measure objectively in any meaningful way. While the amount of data has skyrocketed, the amount of information meaningful to consumers is still very small and confusing.
3. **The level of trust among patients and purchasers continues to ebb lower,** thanks to a barrage of front-page news stories regarding managed care miscues.
4. **Liability issues are growing**. With proposed changes in legislation, Congress may be moving toward granting patients the right to file lawsuits, not only against health plans themselves but even against the corporations who, on behalf of their employees, selected the plans.
5. **The impact of health care spending on productivity is still unknown**. Despite an expenditure of more than 13 percent

of the gross domestic product on health care, the return on investment in human capital is poorly understood and difficult to justify.

6. **Consumer choice is rapidly shrinking**, despite efforts at reform and the desire to place more control in the hands of patients. With health care providers beginning to resemble oligopolies in many locales, the number of plans available and the choices within a particular plan are declining. With less competition, consumers are feeling increasingly vulnerable.

Given these symptoms, it is time to discard the old, traditional way of thinking about health care and take a fresh look at the issues and challenges that face us. I have written this book not only to shed light on what is wrong, but to examine the art of the possible with regard to making things better. The debate over our health care includes complexities and passions found virtually nowhere else in our economy. It also poses some of the most significant challenges we will face as a society.

To tackle these challenges, I will seek to strike a balance among the seemingly disparate disciplines of economics, medicine, technology, and politics. Chapters 1 and 2 of this book are aimed at trying to understand the forces affecting the system — including the demographic, financial and technological challenges — and the impact these forces will have on shaping the new economy and the new social contract and values being created in the workplace.

Chapter 3 provides a historical look at the health care system and its current trajectory.

Chapters 4, 5, 6, and 7 discuss the opportunity to employ technology to reconstruct the delivery system into a far more efficient model by redesigning the care of patients through new technologies and ways of moving information. This new model changes the roles of health care workers, as well as their mission, organization, and compensation.

Chapter 8 examines the treatment of disability as opposed to illness. Disability is an issue the system has long ignored, but it is a very significant and growing component of the challenges we face.

Finally, in Chapter 9, I examine actions that need to be undertaken by purchasers to help the system evolve into a more compassionate and effective one, focused on individual health and the quality and value of care being delivered.

Author

David B. Friend, M.D., MBA, leads Watson Wyatt's consulting operations in the eastern United States and is a member of the firm's Global Management Committee. Dr. Friend also serves on the Board of Directors of Watson Wyatt and is Chairman of the Finance Committee.

Prior to being appointed to his current position, Dr. Friend served as the global director of group and health care consulting for Watson Wyatt. In his consulting capacity, Dr. Friend provides strategic advice concerning the restructuring of the health care industry. His clients include employers, providers, governments and insurers. Dr. Friend has held executive positions at High Voltage Engineering, Bank Boston, Robertson Stephenson and Sanus (now part of Aetna).

Dr. Friend earned a bachelor's degree in economics from Brandeis University, a master's of business administration from The Wharton School of the University of Pennsylvania and a medical doctorate degree from the University of Connecticut School of Medicine. He is a diplomate of the National Board of Medical Examiners and a licensed physician in the state of Massachusetts. He is also a member of the Board of the Institute for Health Policy at The Heller School of Brandeis University. Dr. Friend holds an appointment at Harvard Medical School's Brigham & Women's Hospital where he is a Visiting Scientist at the Innovation Center for Information Technology.

Dr. Friend is a frequently sought out speaker and commentator. He and his wife, Susan, live in the Boston area.

Acknowledgments

I would like to thank my colleagues at Watson Wyatt for their support and research-based thinking. John Menefee was immensely helpful both in conducting original research and writing extensive portions of the manuscript, including chapters 8 and 9, on disability and value purchasing. Sylvester Schieber and his team at Watson Wyatt's Research and Information Center provided many of the charts, graphs, and analyses utilized in the text. Jamie Hale, Ira Kay and Heidi T. Töppel contributed groundbreaking ideas on physician compensation. Randall Abbott and Richard Ostuw patiently reviewed the manuscript for accuracy and consistency. Robert McKee and Gretchen Ace of Watson Wyatt's Marketing Department helped make the book a reality. Carter Prescott, Carter Communications International Inc., served with distinction as my editor, helping me crystallize complicated and often disjointed thinking.

I would also like to thank my former medical and business school professors, who provided me encouragement at critical times in my training: Howard Bailit, Leann Canty, Peter Deckers, Jeffrey Gross, Joseph Healey, June Kinney, Bruce Koeppen, James Quinn, Fred Rickles, and Anthony Voytovich. In addition, several of the research physicians at the Brigham and Women's Hospital Innovation Center for Information Technology, including Jonathan Schaffer, Luke Sato and Robert Greenes deserve special mention for helping me think through the mind-numbing complexity and wondrous possibilities that are embodied in virtual health care.

Finally, I would like to thank my wife, Sue, and my children, Michael, Daniel, and William, for their encouragement and support.

Contents

Illness is the night-side of life, a more onerous citizenship. Everyone who is born holds dual citizenship, in the kingdom of the well and in the kingdom of the sick. Although we all prefer to use only the good passport, sooner or later each of us is obliged, at least for a spell, to identify ourselves as citizens of that other place.

— **Susan Sontag**

chapter one

Three Powerful Forces

*Will you still need me, will you still feed me, when
I'm 64?* *

With the explosion of global commerce triggered by the end of the
Cold War, three secular forces — an aging population, politically
generated financial pressures, and advancing technology — are
rolling through the new world economy with the strength of a
tsunami, unleashing enormous economic and political turmoil in
their wake. As they converge, these forces will render entire areas
of human enterprise virtually unrecognizable from their current
form. This transformation will be at least as profound as was the
industrial revolution on the agrarian-based economy it displaced.

Nowhere will this sea change have more potential than in the
health care arena, which will experience an opportunity to
undergo a quantum leap that could rival the discovery of anes-
thesia or penicillin. This unprecedented opportunity to improve
the human condition is offered by the confluence of scientific discoveries, technological innovation and free-market economics. The
potential to increase the length and quality of life will escalate
dramatically. Yet the new world of health care will not be shaped
by physicians or hospitals alone. Rather, the underpinnings of
tomorrow's health care will be built on competencies including
vendor management, mass customization and virtual health care
technology. Therefore, in order to understand society's options to
meet the challenges of the 21st century, we must first seek to
comprehend the triad of forces that will be shaping the next millennium.

* "When I'm Sixty-Four," John Lennon/Paul McCartney, Copyright© 1967 Sony/ATV Songs
LLC (Renewed). All rights administered by Sony/ATV Music Publishing, 8 Music Square W.,
Nashville, TN 37203. All rights reserved. Used by permission.

1

The Elder Boomer Bulge

The world's population is aging at an unprecedented rate (Figure 1.1), profoundly stressing existing health care systems everywhere. For example, Japan's percent of the population over age 60 will double, to more than 30 percent by 2030. In Italy, the population over 60 in 1990 was already at 20 percent, and that number will nearly double, to 35 percent, by 2030. China, with only eight percent of its population over age 60 in 1990, will experience a near tripling by 2030 — more than 300 million individuals. The United Kingdom is projected to see a one-third increase in its 60+ population by 2030.

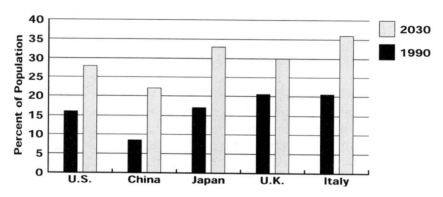

Figure 1.1   Global growth in population over age 60. (Source: Watson Wyatt Worldwide, 1997.)

In the United States alone, someone turns 50 every eight seconds and will continue to do so for the next 10 years. These aging baby boomers, nearly 80 million strong, will total nearly one-third of the U.S. population in the next century. As *The Atlantic Monthly* points out, "By 2025, the proportion of all Americans who are elderly will be the same as the proportion in Florida today. ... America, in effect, will become a nation of Floridas." Figure 1.2 puts this dramatic transformation into stark relief. In the 20-year period from 2010 to 2030, the portion of the U.S. population over age 65 is expected to grow by as much as it had grown in the prior 80 years.

As boomers age, their need for health care will grow almost logarithmically (Figure 1.3). By 2020, this cohort of elder boomers (age 65 and older) will require, on average, six times more health care dollars per capita than they do today. Why? Biology. As

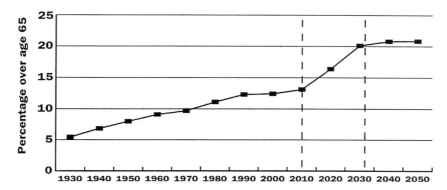

Figure 1.2 Percentage of U.S. population over age 65 for selected years. (Sources: U.S. Bureau of the Census, Historical Statistics of the United States, Colonial Times to 1970, Bicentennial Edition, Part 1 (Washington, D.C., 1975), pp. 8, 10; Social Security Administration, 1995 Annual Report of the Board of Trustees of the Federal Old-Age and Survivors Insurance and Disability Insurance Trust Funds, p. 147.)

humans get older, wear and tear increases the demand for restoration and repair. In fact, according to researchers at Watson Wyatt Worldwide, the health care needs of an older population increase virtually exponentially. On average, a 65-year-old male today consumes six times the amount of health care that he did 40 years ago at age 25. Fifteen years from now, when that male reaches 80 years of age, he will consume 12 times the amount of care that he required as a 25-year-old.

Much of this increase occurs, sadly, because almost half of our citizens over age 85 now suffer from some form of dementia. As this over-80 age group increases in size from three million to over 20 million in the coming decades, the number of people suffering from dementia will skyrocket proportionally. The personal toll on families suffering from the consequences of this disease alone — as well as the financial toll — will be staggering.

Dramatic financial pressures

As the world's elderly population grows, every society on earth will face escalating pressure to finance unavoidable health care needs. Promises made years ago by politicians to provide care forever, when the bulk of the boomer population was young, healthy, and inexpensive, are rapidly becoming unaffordable. One need only look at every major western democracy to see the grow-

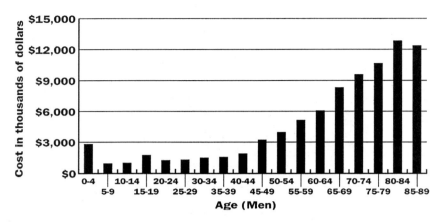

Figure 1.3   Aging and annual health costs. (Source: Watson Wyatt Worldwide estimates based on individual 1995 annual health care expenditures.)

ing inability to satisfy the promises of yesteryear. For example, the Canadian health system and the National Health Service in the United Kingdom are under tremendous economic pressure, having to reduce services and coverage to stave off financial disaster. Civil servants went on strike in France in 1997 because of threats to the health care promise.

It will be no different in the United States. The financial impact of caring for elder boomers will be extraordinary. Escalating growth in the retiree population has only just begun to put enormous financial burdens on entitlement programs for the elderly, such as Social Security and Medicare, as well as on younger workers who will be subsidizing retiree pensions and benefits.

Consider the impact on Medicare. In 1996, for the first time since the program's inception some 30 years ago, Medicare Part A's tax receipts were insufficient to cover the expenses incurred by its current 36 million recipients. While accounting gimmicks can mask the problem for the next few years, they do not solve it. Further, if the U.S. government lacks the political will and is unable to raise enough tax revenue during booming economic times to pay for the needs of 36 million people, how will it find the fortitude to finance the needs of nearly 80 million in the next 20 years?

The Congressional Budget Office projects Medicare spending to grow at an average annual rate of 8.3 percent over the next 10 years. The $208 billion spent on the program last year will more than double to $448 billion in 2008. The cost of Medicare alone will take 16 percent of the federal budget just as the baby-boom generation starts to hit its retirement stride. If these projections hold, Medicare's bill will be more than we now spend for the medical care of the entire population — children, working people and retirees.

Another financial force promising to exacerbate the situation is inflation. Contrary to conventional wisdom, medical inflation is not dead. In fact, while the Consumer Price Index (CPI) has averaged 2.9 percent in the 1990s, the medical CPI has grown nearly 60 percent faster, at 5 percent per year (Table 1.1).

Table 1.1 Consumer and Medical Consumer Price Indices
1979 to 1999[1]

Year	CPI	Annual Percentage Change	Medical CPI	Annual Percentage Change
1979	76.7	–	70.6	—
1980	86.3	12.5%	77.6	9.9%
1981	94	8.9%	87.3	12.5%
1982	97.6	3.8%	96.9	11.0%
1983	101.3	3.8%	103.1	6.4%
1984	105.3	3.9%	109.4	6.1%
1985	109.3	3.8%	116.8	6.8%
1986	110.5	1.1%	125.8	7.7%
1987	115.4	4.4%	133.1	5.8%
1988	120.5	4.4%	142.3	6.9%
1989	126.1	4.6%	154.4	8.5%
1990	133.8	6.1%	169.2	9.6%
1991	137.9	3.1%	182.6	7.9%
1992	141.9	2.9%	194.7	6.6%
1993	145.8	2.7%	205.2	5.4%
1994	149.7	2.7%	215.3	4.9%
1995	153.5	2.5%	223.8	3.9%
1996	158.6	3.3%	230.6	3.0%
1997	161.3	1.7%	237.1	2.8%
1998	163.9	1.6%	245.2	3.4%
1999[1]	165.0	1.8%	248.3	3.9%

[1] Estimated based on first-quarter results.

Source: Consumer Price Index, 1913–present, Bureau of Labor Statistics, April, 1999.

Worse still, given the rapid developments in expensive medical technology and new pharmaceuticals, combined with demographically driven demand and the growing tendency of health care to engage in oligopolistic practices, the likelihood of medical inflation's increasing is far greater than popularly believed.

If these trends hold, they will further burden our severely under-funded health care system. At a minimum, health care premiums will rise. Between increased costs and the gradual reneging of past political promises, we believe that the number of uninsured people in the United States could increase from 40 million to more than 60 million in the next few years as cost increases price health insurance out of the reach of millions.

These trends also will create a daunting challenge for employers and their employees. The first baby boomers will start qualifying for early retirement in less than five years, when they begin turning 55. With the specter of the Medicare eligibility age's being raised to age 67 and beyond to control government outlays, the gap between the termination of employer-sponsored medical benefits, as active workers retire, and the restarting of Medicare benefits could exceed a decade or more. This period of time will leave new retirees and their families naked with regard to health care coverage, just as biology starts to demand its due. Employers who pay for the health benefits of early retirees until they qualify for Medicare will be paying twice the bill compared with retirees who are Medicare eligible. The likelihood that employers will continue to absorb these costs for large numbers of new retirees is doubtful.

Regardless of the level of employer-sponsored retiree health benefits that are offered, a growing cost burden will fall on active workers. Because employers typically do not prefund retiree benefits, the costs must be paid for from current revenue generated by the hard work of active employees. Such pay-as-you-go financing, combined with corporate downsizing and an aging population, will dramatically increase the cost burden on the next generation of employees. In fact, the cost of providing health insurance to retirees could easily exceed $10,000 for each salaried worker and $20,000 for each hourly worker every year of their working life.

This claim against the future output of the workforce will create tremendous financial pressure to significantly curtail, if not completely abandon, the provision of employer-sponsored retiree health benefits. The temptation to dramatically reduce or jettison such plans — and leave retired employees without coverage — is already enormous. Not surprisingly, many corporations have already begun to do so. As both corporations and government shrink from their commitments, the most fortunate employees will be faced with the choice of deferring retirement or suffering reduced benefits. Unlucky or low-skilled workers will likely be frozen out of retiree benefits entirely, left to fend for their health care entirely on their own.

Surprisingly, many employers believe they have already addressed the coming problem by implementing Financial Accounting Standard 106,* but this is simply an accounting convention, not a solution; it does not address the real issue of whether companies will have the cash to continually pay these obligations. While the government has the option of seemingly being able to borrow forever without repaying its debt, corporations cannot. Further, while companies can renege on past promises, such behavior does not create a climate of trust that helps attract and retain current employees. Offering a "deal" that asks employees to devote their lives to the organization and in return, just as their moment of need arrives for health care, abandons them to fend for themselves, does not appear to be a winning strategy in the coming war for talent.

Thus, we have the first two of many paradoxical promises. The first is made by employers to attract and retain current employees. It goes like this: devote your energies to the corporation while you are healthy and productive. In return, the company promises it will take care of you when you are no longer productive (i.e., retired) and start to consume more health care dollars (i.e., you get older). The second promise is made by government to induce the population to voluntarily surrender some of its pay. It goes like this: Pay taxes to the government when you are healthy and productive. In return, the government promises to spend money on you when you are no longer able to work or pay taxes and need care.

The problem is that neither the government nor employers can seem to afford to keep these promises. The paradox is that they cannot afford to go back on them, either. What they hope is — over time — to default in a stealthy manner, hoping that no one will notice.

This obfuscation strategy is unlikely to succeed. Business leaders and politicians must deal with these issues, and the sooner the better. Companies need to assess their current programs against a range of politically expedient reforms that may turn into legislation. They should seek to maximize the value received for every

---

* FAS 106, Employers' Accounting for Postretirement Benefits Other Than Pensions, was issued in 1990. FAS 106 primarily affects accounting for postretirement medical and life insurance benefits. It is based on the finding by FASB (Financial Accounting Standards Board) that postretirement medical and life insurance benefits are a form of deferred compensation, the costs of which should be accrued over the period in which employees render the services necessary to earn the benefits.

dollar spent on health care. While capping retiree health benefits may be inevitable, employers need to encourage the growth of more-efficient health care systems by rewarding the more efficient providers with their business. Further, companies and government need to be honest. They need to tell the population that they must save for retirement themselves, and as they do so, they need to factor in the cost of health care as part of their overall retirement planning. However, this may be strong medicine to a population that is still woefully unprepared for its future.

Technological advances

As Jack Welch, chief executive officer of General Electric, likes to make clear, "The world will change more in the next 10 years than in the last 100 years." Nowhere is this truer than in the rapidly advancing field of technology, the third dynamic force for change.

As Nicholas Negroponte explains in his book, *Being Digital*, electron-based technologies now allow the transformation of information from atoms to bits — from the physical book you are reading now to the zeroes and ones of digital communication. That means the entire contents of this book, words and graphics alike, can be transported at the speed of light through a wireless or landline telecommunications link to be read on a hand-held computerized book at the click of a button. The same is true for X-rays, EKGs, ultrasounds and all other sorts of medical information. Since health care is largely a transaction based on the transfer of information, for the first time in history geographic distance is no longer a barrier to receiving health care.

Those rushing electrons can power the globalization of medical care, making it readily available anytime, anywhere, to anyone. With electronic data moved instantaneously and inexpensively, medical information can become universally accessible. Health care can become portable, freed from geographic constraint. The informatics revolution potentially makes the knowledge and skills of every health care professional on the planet accessible to the entire population simultaneously. By combining this level of access with local centers of production, the opportunity to create health care that is produced in mass, but customized to the needs of the individual, is upon us.

As the possibility of global medical practice becomes real, the question becomes, will societies and legislatures — which for centuries have controlled medicine on a geographical basis — open their borders? Once doctors can sit in Boston and read X-rays in London, how viable will the British National Health Service's monopoly to provide care remain? Once a doctor possesses technology that allows the treatment of individuals anywhere on the globe, medical commerce will be altered forever. The concept of local licensing boards will resemble 13th-century guilds in their obsolescence, attempting, as King Canute did, to hold back the tide of progress.

Thus another paradox emerges: The practice of medicine will increasingly move one foot into the 21st century through technology, while the other will be stuck in the 13th century through its policies and guild-like thinking.

With information technology providing the opportunity to practice medicine smarter and better, simultaneous developments in molecular biology, genetics, pharmaceuticals, medical devices, and biotechnology mean that a greater proportion of illness will either be eliminated or moved from an acute and potentially lethal condition to one that is chronic and long-lived.

For instance, acute illnesses such as heart disease, which traditionally had a short duration and fatal consequences, is being converted into a chronic disease with less catastrophic, but more long-term consequences. Though this conversion represents a blessing to patients in terms of both the quantity and quality of life they bring, the result is a dramatic increase in the cost of care. Instead of paying for a short, intense period of care for an ultimately fatal heart attack, society is faced with the challenge of *providing and paying* for short periods of intensive care followed by a multi-decade course of rehabilitation, medication, and maintenance. Another example of such a phenomenon is impotence, seemingly incurable for many. Now it may be reversible through new drugs such as Viagra. The possibilities, as well as the costs, will be nearly limitless.

Another area of technological revolution that is occurring is in the field of medical informatics. If an army is equipped with $25 fiber-optic, sensor-laden T-shirts, soldiers shot in the field can be diagnosed just after they hit the ground. The location and nature of their bullet wounds, the diagnosis of life-threatening arterial vs. less serious wounds, can be determined by a central medical clinic staffed with experts, in real time. Experts believe this technology has the potential to reduce battlefield deaths by up to 50 percent. Consider the impact of using similar technology in the home or in an airplane, where a passenger traveling at 30,000 feet can have his chest pain diagnosed as if he were in a hospital's emergency room on terra firma. The power of information to be delivered in a far more efficient and accurate form dramatically expands the potential availability, quantity, and quality of medical care.

But technology will cause its own set of pressures. More people living longer with chronic health conditions will be an expensive proposition. The circular relationship between technology and the demands of the population for health insurance coverage will push health care costs even higher. Patients today insist on the most advanced and expensive treatment possible, and they are demanding that insurance cover their costs. The result is that the developers and practitioners of expensive new technologies have an enormous incentive to continue to push the envelope, no matter how effective or ineffective their products turn out to be. This is one of the reasons that fascinating technology has come into being. But paradoxically, it is also one of the reasons the medical system is facing insolvency.

For example, financial motivation drives the pharmaceutical industry to continue to create an extraordinary pipeline of new discoveries to help reduce the effects of aging on baby boomers. The success of new drugs such as Prilosec for ulcers, Zocor and Lipitor to reduce cholesterol, Novasac to reduce blood pressure, Paxil for depression, Claritin and Flonase for allergies, Zyprexa for schizophrenia and Rezulin for diabetes, simply stimulates the demand for more on the part of both the consuming public and the drug industry. Drug spending alone in the U.S. has doubled from just five years ago, to over $100 billion in 1998 and the trend appears to be accelerating (Table 1.2).

Table 1.2 Who Pays for Prescriptions

	1990	1995	1998
Patient	63%	38.2%	25%
Medicaid	10.7%	12.7%	10.4%
Third Party	26.1%	49.1%	64.5%

It is neither possible nor desirable to stop the advance of technology. As Negroponte points out, "The change from atoms to bits is irrevocable and unstoppable." But we must learn how to best harness and implement technology to equitably distribute and finance the fruits of that innovation.

All together now

The combined impact of demographics, financial demands and rapidly developing technology are certain to increase future health care expenditures dramatically in the United States. Left unchecked, Watson Wyatt believes that health care spending will more than triple within the next 30 years. Failure to respond to this coming tidal wave will have century-long consequences. More people will go uncovered, particularly in older age groups. The impact will be especially hard on people between ages 55 and 70, as they are cast off from their employers at the same time as the government defaults on its promise to provide care. Those falling into the ranks of the uninsured will require additional employer tax revenues to subsidize their care. As a final irony, raising the eligibility age for Medicare might tempt employees to postpone their retirement, meaning extra years of health care cost responsibility for their employers.

From a public funding perspective, the government will be forced to increase payroll taxes significantly. Medicare tax rates as a percentage of payroll have historically been relatively low. First set in 1966 at about one percent each for workers and employers, they have only risen to 1.45 percent respectively over the past 30 years. But to fund the projected cost of current promises (not including the cost of paying for Social Security), Medicare tax rates will need to be increased almost eight-fold — to 12 percent each, for employees and their corporations, between 2010 and 2030 — just to pay for elder boomers in retirement.

The vicious circle of cost shifting is now likely to enter a new, more aggressive, and sophisticated era. Except for the United States and South Africa, where health care finance is primarily the responsibility of the employer, it is currently government's obligation in the rest of the world. As we enter the next millennium, it should come as no surprise that governments around the world will try to renege on their promises and shift the cost toward employers and workers. Consider yourself forewarned. This issue will be around long after Y2K is forgotten.

In the United States, efforts are already under way to shift costs at the federal level, albeit gingerly. Inquiring how the country will finance and supply health care in the future has long been the "third rail" of American politics. Things appear little changed from the early 1800s, when Lord Byron wrote, "It is very iniquitous to make me pay my debts — you have no idea of the pain it gives one." Or perhaps American politicians have taken to heart Ralph Waldo Emerson's words: "Solvency is maintained by means of a national debt, on the principle, 'If you will not lend me the money, how can I pay you?'"

But the fact remains that the political system has saddled American society with an actuarially unsound health policy compounded by a pay-as-you-go mechanism in which tomorrow's generation is saddled with today's health care bill. Unlike pension savings, which had previously suffered from this dilemma and enjoyed at least partial rectification by the political process through the Employee Retirement Income Security Act (ERISA), there has been no corresponding solution for health care.

With ERISA, only half of the "retirement problem" was ever addressed. Pensions are clearly necessary for retirement but are no longer sufficient. Resources to pay for health care are also required to enjoy one's "golden years." Not only has the U.S. government failed to put aside money for health care, employers and elder boomers are equally culpable. A recent study of 1,000 50-year-olds who planned to retire by age 63 found that average respondents expected to have saved a total of $140,000 to live on for the rest of their lives. With the average U.S. life expectancy now in excess of age 80, these individuals are likely to have enough trouble paying for food and rent, let alone for their ever-increasing health care needs.

So who *is* going to pay? The 1996 Presidential campaign, the recent failure of the 1999 Medicare Commission to reach consensus, and subsequent budget agreements demonstrate how politically difficult it is today to grapple with these issues by proposing either to raise taxes or cut benefits. As a result of the current political climate, we believe three trends will continue to unfold. First, the federal government will follow its trend to slowly shift much of the cost increases to state governments. The current welfare reform program provides an excellent guide as to how this can be done. Second, federal and state governments will carry on shifting the cost burden to corporations in the form of higher taxes and user fees. A good example of this trend is provided by New York State, which deregulated its hospital industry on January 1, 1997, and, not coincidentally, found that it could, through a series of user fees and taxes, raise over $2 billion in additional revenue from corporations. Third, costs will go on being moved to providers in the form of reduced payments. Medicare proposals to decrease payments for residency training, or for supplying items such as oxygen, are good examples.

Faced with the new political impossibilities of raising taxes or cutting benefits, we expect the U.S. government to attempt to elegantly turn its back on its past promises and pass on more costs to the states, private corporations, providers, and citizens. Perhaps predicted and actual budget surpluses will encourage more forthright discussion. However, if history is any guide, this appears unlikely.

The consequences of these changes will be a wholesale rewrite of the underlying social contract. The promise of a defined benefit pension check, along with complete access and payment for health care, will be replaced by a defined contribution pension plan, where a set amount of money will be provided, regardless of its adequacy, to pay for the quality of life expected and the level of health care needed. No matter how this sleight of hand is conducted, it will result in broken promises the world over. Politicians and employers have promised more than they can afford to deliver. This game of medical-cost hot potato will only accelerate. Unfortunately, it may serve only to rearrange the deck furniture on the *Titanic,* not alter its course.

chapter two

New Deal, New Values

> *The marginal value of investing in human perfor-*
> *mance is about three times greater than the value of*
> *investing in machinery.* *

The social contract between government and its citizens is not the
only agreement being rewritten in an effort to overcome the challenges posed by demographics, finance, and technology. The ability to redefine and manage the evolving relationship between
employers and employees has become an essential strategy in the
global battle to build sustainable competitive advantage.

Like governments, businesses around the world are saddled
with past promises that are no longer affordable. As a result,
employers are rethinking the "social contract" they offer employees in return for work. Nowhere is this change more substantial
and emotionally charged than in the area of health care.

Health care represents one of the most visible and expensive
components of the social contract today. Prior to the world's being
engulfed by global capitalism, the social contract was based on a
generally paternalistic affectation on the part of buyers — governments and corporations — toward their employees and citizens,
thereby creating an entitlement culture. For corporations, this
paternalism was fueled by the link between compensation and
reporting relationships. Managers sought to maximize the number
of people working for them because their pay was based largely
on the number of employees under their direct supervision.

This paternalistic culture, reinforced by the reward structure,
affected every detail of corporate and civic life, including health

---

* Thomas A. Stewart, *Intellectual Capital: the New Wealth of Organizations*, Doubleday / Currency,
New York, 1997.

care. With health care, employees came to believe they were enti-
tled to Cadillac-like medical care, delivered anytime, any place,
from any doctor and hospital of their choosing, for any reason and
for virtually no cost. The paternalistic social contract gave patients
the power to choose their care and, at the same time, remain
insulated from its true cost.

The dictum has now changed. The old entitlement culture has
collided head-on with the new economic realities of global competition. Managers are now paid to maximize shareholder value
instead of maximizing employment. Under the new rules, purchasers can no longer afford to issue blank checks on behalf of their
employees. Investors and taxpayers have begun to hold their corporate and government officials accountable for their level of
health care expenditures and are demanding that they act as pru-
dent fiduciaries, not paternalistic benefactors.

In response, employers have begun to rewrite the social contract. By the mid-1990s, the social contract regarding health care
had been turned on its head. Employers began to drive their
employees toward Yugo-like health care, effectively preventing
patients/employees from having a say in their health care decisions.

Further fueling the change in the social contract was the accept-
able practice of shielding the top-level executives making these
decisions from the personal consequences of their decisions. Special gold-plated health programs and other wealth-creation devices
enabled executives to bypass the rationing schemes provided for
their own employees. While such forms of discrimination were
previously considered unacceptable under the old social contract,
which called for equality and equity of health care for all, it has
become as permissible to discriminate in this area as it has in pay,
stock options, and other aspects of compensation. As individual
pay for performance has gained ground and a winner-take-all
mentality has taken root, changes once considered unthinkable in
the social contract now have become commonplace, and every
aspect, including health care, has been altered forever.

Clearly, given the migration from maximizing employment to
maximizing shareholder value, the social contract that binds
employees to employers and governments to their citizenry is in a
state of flux. The prospect of lifetime employment is no longer economically viable to managers attempting to maximize shareholder
value and thus has vanished in many industries. While many purchasers still feel strong social obligations toward their employees,

the trend is inexorable: The ties that bind are weakening; customized pay for performance and tailored deals are gaining strength. In fact, a colleague at Watson Wyatt, Ira T. Kay, argues quite cogently that it is these very pay-for-performance programs that are vital for helping our clients win the global economic war. Maximizing shareholder value is now the predominant directive of companies based in the United States. European companies are clearly moving in that direction, while Japanese corporations are still stuck in the mode of maximizing employment. Paradoxically, the commitment toward maximizing employment, enforced through heavy-handed, government-mandated benefit programs, may, in fact, have done the opposite and held back Japan's economy and also contributed to Europe's failure to create additional jobs in the 1970s and 1980s. Meanwhile, the United States, with its economy focused on shareholder value, has been the job-creation envy of the world, with 24.7 million new jobs created between 1980 and 1996.

If shareholder value is the Holy Grail, then why shouldn't we be cheering the demise of the old deal? Perhaps we should. Employers are looking for new flexibility from their employees, and those employees are expecting a new reward structure in turn. The revised social contract, however, is at best a work in progress and generally not yet in place, so both sides are pulling in vastly different directions. Such misalignment between labor and the strategic goals of corporations is resulting in turnover, foregone productivity, and a serious loss of morale.

If future profit growth is to take place from deriving more value from intellectual (human) capital, then numerous problems only now simmering may be brought to full boil when companies attempt to fully leverage their employees and find they fall short because the necessary worker commitment is not there. Proof of this can be seen in a 1997 Watson Wyatt study of 1,000 employers across North America. It showed that the most financially successful companies were those that created an environment rewarding performance and personal growth and, as a result, enjoyed the highest commitment levels among their employees.

What drives the cartoon character Dilbert into becoming the star of three business books appearing simultaneously on *The New York Times* best-seller list? It may be that most corporations, through their inadequate structural capital, utilize only a small fraction of their employees' mental capacity at work. The result is frustrated employees. The antidote to "Dilbertitis" could be to create structural capital that generates an environment where people can reach their full potential. This direction of structural and human capital is likely to become one of the major management challenges of the next century, one where success in this regard will be the source of enormous competitive advantage.

One of the other key drivers enabling employees to reach their full potential will be their health. The issue of health benefits arouses enormous passion between employees and employers and is a critical component of many corporate social contracts. Yet health care policies often inconsistently deal with many applications that are neither consistent nor logical. While paternalistic in one area, such as acute health needs, they are totally silent on other areas, such as disability. This phenomenon is not uncommon. In fact, 58 percent of the companies surveyed in 1998 by Watson Wyatt and the Washington Business Group on Health do not integrate disability benefits into employee health plans. Such inconsistency is often the result of a lack of strategic health focus. The consequence is a mixed message that makes employees confused and cynical and employers frustrated and angry.

What, then, is the ultimate effect of misaligned programs and mixed messages? It is diminished competitive advantage. Any time your intellectual assets feel they are being treated unfairly — a natural assumption, given that the old deal is being ripped up before their eyes with its replacement still unclear — intellectual capacity cannot be fully leveraged. And make no mistake about it: *Whoever leverages brainpower the best will win*. Or, to quote from *The Leadership Engine* by Noel Tichy and Eli Cohen: "The competitor with the most leaders at the most levels wins."

The importance of intellectual capital

In our current economic environment, no company or government can afford even the perception of shabby treatment of employees who have spent their careers honing their intellectual capital. Encouraging intellectual capital to attain peak physical and mental conditions is critical to making sure that employees show up at work engaged and operating at full potential. Maintaining a robust level of health within the intellectual capital base will become a key competitive core competency for many high-performance organizations.

Whether a company makes widgets or chips, its greatest assets walk out the door every night. Brainpower and knowledge are easily transportable. Therefore, attracting, retaining, and maintaining these assets in a healthy state and keeping them fully productive become top priorities.

For employees, one of the most important parts of the social contract is their health care coverage, for it enables them to better maximize their full potential. Organizations that keep their employees healthy are likely to enjoy sustainable competitive advantage. This requires employers to consider the strategic implications of health benefits for two reasons — they need to attract and retain talent, and they need to keep that talent operating at peak efficiency.

Organizations wishing to outsource the provision of health care can consider a variety of alternatives. One is converting their defined benefit health plans to a defined contribution arrangement where only the employer's contributions are defined, not the actual health benefit. Employee leasing is a variation on this theme. Each of these alternatives, however, carries a significant risk for survival in an increasingly competitive business arena. Shareholders may not be willing to pay as much for the stock of corporations whose earnings are contingent on non-proprietary intellectual capital. Investors may be far more likely to pay a premium for the right to own those organizations that can amass, organize, and leverage intellectual capital on a proprietary basis.

As health care benefits are transformed to become a tool for workforce management, they have the potential to become key strategic weapons in the battle for human capital. Though purchasing health care may become increasingly complicated in the years to come, mastery of it may become essential for corporate success.

Is intellectual capital the only resource that will allow companies to maintain a sustainable competitive advantage? Many organizations point to other assets on which they rely, such as local geography, natural resources, access to capital markets, or political systems. Yet with the rapid globalization of the economy, all these other barriers or advantages are fading; the playing field is becoming more level. Thus, brainpower and the capacity to keep it healthy and effectively deployed may become the *sine qua non* of business success.

Three elements to master

To maximize their intellectual capital, the future prospects of virtually all organizations will rest on their ability to harness three elements:

1. They will need to be excellent *managers* of people (intellectual capital).
2. They will need to master *technology* (structural capital) to best leverage human capital.
3. They will need to understand *finance* (financial capital) to craft a new social contract and reward structure that works for both the organization and its employees.

Changes in attitude toward the importance of healthy intellectual resources will be powered by investors' demand on corporations to continue to grow earnings. Since earnings growth drives stock prices higher, earnings are the Holy Grail. The engine driving corporate earnings growth over the last 10 years has not been labor, but rather the substitute of capital for labor. The key to future earnings, however, may be the ability to increase productivity. The ability to raise productivity may be contingent on the ability of organizations to use technology to leverage brainpower. That leverage will be achieved by organizations skilled at blending management, technology, and financial know-how.

Wall Street is beginning to understand this. Netscape is a prime example. At the time of its initial public offering (IPO), Netscape's balance sheet was $12 million, but its IPO value was $2 billion. Clearly, the marketplace was betting on the superior performance of Netscape's human and other intangible assets. As Thomas A. Stewart notes in his remarkable book, *Intellectual Capital: The New Wealth of Organizations*, "When the stock market values companies at three, four or 10 times the book value of their assets, it's telling a simple but profound truth: The hard assets of a knowledge company contribute far less to the value of its ultimate product (or service) than the intangible assets — the talents of its people, the efficacy of its management systems, the character of its relationships to its customers — that together are its intellectual capital."

Look at Microsoft, another brainpower-rich company. Take Microsoft's market value of approximately $400 billion, as of August 1999. Subtract the value of tangible assets of $16.8 billion. Divide that by the number of employees, roughly 30,000, and you discover that each employee represents a market capitalization of over $12 million to shareholders. If that employee becomes sick and unable to work, Microsoft shareholders could arguably be diminished by well over $10 million. What is it worth for Microsoft to keep that person healthy and working at peak efficiency? If health care is analogous to the cost of maintaining a capital asset, maintenance is justifiable as long as the financial returns are compelling. Skimping on maintenance, while tempting in the short term, is unlikely to provide superior economic returns in the long run.

Ignoring, for a moment, the moral value of health care and simply taking a purely capitalistic perspective, it is just smart business to take care of employees and it is plain dumb to neglect them. If a company buys cheap, inadequate medical care and, as a result, its employees receive substandard care, the company may suffer a depletion of intellectual capital and a diminished stock price. Reporting to investors in its annual report that $100 was saved on medical tests but $100,000 worth of intellectual capital became inoperable as a result, is not likely to impress shareholders.

Since companies cannot own brainpower as they can bricks and mortar, they will be compelled to develop innovative ways to rent it. The lease terms will be represented by the new social contract. The ability of management to effectively leverage an organization's perpetually leased intellectual capital to create maximum shareholder value may become the gold standard for evaluating management's effectiveness. Managing the health of employees is likely to show up on an increasing number of executives' report cards.

chapter three

From Wastecare to Hollowcare

*My doctor gave me six months to live, but when I couldn't pay the bill, he gave me six months more.**

The manner in which health care is paid for has undergone many incarnations, but the end result is now a delivery system that has become progressively sicker.

Until the 1930s, U.S. consumers paid for health care out of their own pockets. If patients had money, they received treatment. If they didn't have money, they either went without care or received free treatment from their physicians. During World War II, with wage freezes established, corporations increasingly began to offer additional benefits in lieu of pay increases. One of the most significant benefits available to offer was health insurance.

The offer of health care, however, marked the beginning of the bifurcation between the patient and the purchaser of care. The benefit was inexpensive, since the working population was young and healthy. Also contributing to the benefit's low cost was the technological reality at the time: Medicine was largely unable to have an impact on disease. As the old medical school adage went, "One-third of the time the doctor makes things better, one-third of the time the doctor makes things worse and one-third of the time the doctor has no impact, and we are never sure of what time it is." This sentiment, largely accepted within the temple of medicine, was seldom discussed with the public. Hospital care was rare because, by and large, little good could actually be done in hospitals.

* Walter Matthau

This benign cost environment began to change in the 1950s and 1960s. Medical science started to make substantial advances, allowing physicians to develop meaningful treatments. Kidney dialysis, transplant surgery, antibiotics, heart-lung machines, and other breakthroughs changed the course of medicine and added an expensive technological and information basis to health care. The Hill-Burton Act promoted the construction of high-tech tertiary medical centers to house scientifically based physicians. The locus of health care delivery migrated from the house call and the individual doctor's office to the medical center.

Hospitals became vertically integrated, offering all things to all people because unsophisticated buyers who had a price-is-no-object mentality funded them. Insulated from market forces, medical centers were encouraged to be inefficient. The more inefficient they were, the more money they made. When patients broke a hip, they would receive all of their services in a critical care hospital, including the operation as well as the pharmacy services and rehabilitation, regardless of how inefficiently these services were delivered. Like department stores, hospitals offered everything, including centralized access to patients' medical records and to specialists of every stripe. Far from serving the needs of patients, medical centers became designed for the ease of the specialist physicians, who usually maintained their offices nearby. Primary care providers generally were not welcome, often kept out of the "temple" and forced to set up shop outside the hospital walls.

Simultaneously, employers began turning to insurance companies to handle the growing complexity of the medical system. These large insurers, acting as financial intermediaries, created greater distance between patients and buyers and their providers. The federal government mimicked the private sector by offering medical insurance to the uninsured through Medicare and Medicaid, acting only as the intermediary.

The net result was that the old marketplace, composed of millions of individual transactions between patients and doctors, was transformed into one where large companies and governments began to buy care from large medical systems using financial intermediaries to handle the exchange. The companies, insurers, and hospitals assumed the roles of buyers and sellers in a marketplace where those functions previously had been embodied in the patient–doctor relationship.

As purchasers paid premiums to the insurers, the insurers retained a portion of that money for their administrative costs and the risk associated with payment of claims, passing on the rest of the funds to the medical centers and physicians in a relatively unmanaged environment. The net effect of the branching between the payers and the patients in the system, combined with massive government stimulus, was the destruction of anything resembling a functioning capital allocation market mechanism for the buying and selling of medical goods and services.

The binge begins

In economics, we are taught that marketplaces are a collection of opinions, influences, and competing distortions, all serving one primary purpose — to allot scarce resources. Markets, by their very nature, seek to maximize return on invested capital by allocating capital to suppliers that profitably and effectively service and attract customers. Therefore, the power of the marketplace to shape providers and their behavior is enormous. Such was the case with the health care delivery system. Purchasers of health care — namely governments and private corporations — exerted enormous influence over the health care delivery system because they, not the patients themselves, collectively paid the bills.

The twin effects of disconnecting the patient from having to pay for care and government legislation encouraging the creation of new tertiary medical capacity dramatically increased the demand for care and the amount of money available to satisfy its cost. This effectively lowered investment barriers, causing a great deal of wasteful investment in unneeded capacity, especially among acute care hospitals and specialists. At the same time, the reduction of the investment barriers for tertiary care crowded out investment in primary care. The result was an explosion in the availability of investment, not for primary care but for more unneeded capacity in tertiary and specialty care.

With investment dollars available, the gold rush was on. The country went on a medical capacity-expansion binge that brought on an enormous increase in high-tech hospitals and doctors trained in expensive procedures. This gave way to a system whose gears became stuck in production mode, pumping out supply long after baseline needs had been met, creating serious imbalances between supply and demand. The net effect of this unneeded capacity was a wasteful and inefficient health care system we call "Wastecare."

Wastecare's generic approach to medical problems was to use a sledgehammer when a fly swatter would do. Back pain, for example, was no longer treated first with bed rest for a few days but with MRIs and exotic medications. Specialists treated colds with fancy antibiotics. Expensive tests and procedures were preferred over listening or talking to patients. Cognitive thinking took a back seat to procedures. Tertiary care was encouraged for primary care situations. Children's hospitals, designed for rare and unusual diseases, proliferated in such numbers that more than 80 percent of their day-to-day business became driven not by tertiary conditions but by primary needs such as asthma.

Due to the distortion in the market's internal capital allocation mechanism in favor of Wastecare, the system encouraged and rewarded its own proliferation while punishing the alternative. Identical investments in medical school tuition and study generated a far higher return for medical students electing to become specialists long after the supply of specialists had exceeded any reasonable need. Meanwhile, the pursuit of general medicine was discouraged, even though clear shortages existed.

Because Wastecare was virtually written into statute and normal market-clearing mechanisms were not allowed to function, there was no real market mechanism to shut off the production. Had a functioning market-clearing mechanism been in place, returns on investment would have been lowered appropriately in areas of excess capacity by the laws of supply and demand and increased in fields experiencing a shortage.

Instead, the imbalance continued to grow unabated despite obvious supply and demand dynamics. The best and brightest were encouraged to continue on in specialties. "Doing well for yourself by doing well for others" was the refrain. Life for doctors who became specialists was close to nirvana.

But the growing waste and misapplication of resources was bad for society. Ironies abounded. For example, few doctors wanted to invest their human capital and train to become experts in geriatrics, despite overwhelming demographic demand and virtually no supply, because the broken market allocation mechanism generated such poor salaries and such a poor return on their human capital investment.

Draining the system

This systematic, long-term, wasteful allocation of human and financial capital resulted in a totally misaligned and inefficient health care delivery system. By the late 1980s, the system began to require ever-increasing quantities of money to overcome its built-in inefficiencies and still provide the government-decreed returns on invested capital.

At the same time, the single fastest-growing expense category for corporations became health care costs.* To exacerbate the problem, a deep economic recession developed in the late 1980s, along with rapidly escalating medical inflation. If unabated, this situation would soon threaten the very survival of a significant portion of American industry. For many companies, health care expenses exceeded their bottom lines and, if left unchecked, threatened to consume them.

The threat created a demand for relief among private-sector payers. That relief eventually came, not from the transformation of the medical profession itself, which refused virtually all efforts to change, but in the form of managed care. Created in the early 1970s by the Health Maintenance Organization Act of 1972, managed care companies did not hit their stride until the 1980s. At that time, demands for cost control became critical to the very survival of private corporate payers, whose overseas rivals had cheap labor and subsidized national health care systems providing care at little or no direct costs.

Because they were willing to take on the Wastecare system when traditional insurers and organized medicine would not, managed care companies effectively profited by arbitraging Wastecare. They helped weed out unneeded and inefficient care, shifted costs to the unmanaged payers (chiefly the federal government), and gained price concessions from suppliers who were in vast oversupply. As a result, managed care succeeded by interjecting itself into the marketplace and promising to actually control health care spending.

To fulfill their promises, managed care companies began to impose constraints on the utilization of resources. Coupled with advances in technology, dramatic reductions occurred in the use of hospitalization and other services. In 1960, for example, heart attacks had been thought to require approximately six weeks' of hospital care. Through the impetus of managed care, hospitals and physicians were compelled to more fully understand their treatment processes. In combination with newer drugs and technologies, the length of stay shrank to approximately one week.** This was unlikely to have come about without managed care organiza-

---

* More than 10 years later, the cost of health care benefits still represents the largest component in the price of many products. In the auto industry, for example, the single biggest portion of a car's price is not the glass or steel or rubber but the $800 per car that represents health care benefits for autoworkers.

tions prodding providers to find cheaper treatment methods. Cataract surgery, which 20 years ago called for approximately 10 days of in-hospital head immobilization as standard medical protocol, became an outpatient occurrence. Half-completed hospital wings, built to house large numbers of people lying in an immobilized state, became worthless, although the bonds sold to erect their steel skeletons still had to be paid.

Thrown into a survival mode, hospitals began banding together to ward off competitive pressures, a trend that has accelerated as suppliers move toward oligopoly. Columbia/HCA Healthcare Corporation put together the world's largest investor-owned hospital company in less than a decade. On a smaller scale, prestigious academic medical centers merged — for example, Columbia Presbyterian Medical Center and New York Hospital–Cornell Medical Center, Harvard's Massachusetts General Hospital and Brigham and Women's Hospital, Stanford University Hospital and the University of California at San Francisco.

Through advances in medical technology and financial pressure to find newer, cheaper and faster ways of providing treatment, the 1980s became a period when managed care companies began to reduce the historical escalation of medical costs. Guaranteed by law the right to charge the same prices as the traditional insurers who were not controlling costs in any significant fashion, managed care companies were able to shadow-price less efficient suppliers while cutting costs and keeping the profits for themselves. Meanwhile, purchasers who had been conditioned to whopping increases in annual premiums were seduced by managed care's promise of lower price increases. The net result of this government-approved shadow pricing was that the operating margins and stock prices of managed care concerns swelled dramatically. Rather than rebate the majority of those savings to payers, managed care companies were allowed by statute to divert the money into their shareholders' pockets. While this was being played out, however, the health care delivery infrastructure itself slowly became starved for capital, with deteriorating resources available for clinical care and patient treatment.

At first, the managed care value proposition was easy to deliver. The fruit hung pretty low on the tree. So much waste had been in the system that savings could be found by using fairly

---

** In the United Kingdom today, Emergency Room physicians actually advise some patients who have had minor heart attacks to be treated at home as opposed to being hospitalized because studies show that the outcomes are no different.

painless rationing. By reducing the glaringly wasteful consumption of hospital days and the inappropriate use of specialists and by imposing gatekeepers and other barriers to access, managed care companies were able to achieve limited, though mostly impressive, one-time gains.

Had this effort been honestly marketed and sold for what it was, it would have been recognized as an interim step in the evolution of more efficient care. Unfortunately, that was not the case. Rather than marketing themselves as cost managers and rationers capable of creating one-time improvements, managed care companies cloaked themselves as permanent, efficient, compassionate providers of care.

While this claim created impressive one-time cash flows, the companies chose to market them as annuity-like earnings to drive up their price-to-earnings ratios and stock prices, rather than plow the cash back into clinical core competencies, such as patient care management, communication, human factor design and information technology. Without these fundamental investments, the managed care companies would never be able to fulfill their promises for an extended period. Returns resulting from the one-time picking of low-hanging fruit had been sold to Wall Street as a permanent harvest.

The dawn of Hollowcare

By the mid-1990s, purchasers began recognizing that they were not receiving the efficient managed care they had been promised and paying for from their new health care vendors — the managed care companies. The Wastecare they had received in the 1980s had not been replaced by the Efficientcare they had been promised, but by Hollowcare, so named because the system was hollowed out in an effort to make it cheaper, cheaper, cheaper, while masquerading as efficient.

Hollowcare was the driving force that sent patients home from hospitals before they were ready to go and without adequate support at home to take care of them. Stories of 65-year-olds discharged too soon from the hospital — going home to be taken care of by 75-year-old spouses for an illness that home health care wouldn't cover — became all too real.

Hollowcare was the end product of a squeezed lemon, resulting from the same old, tired managed-cost approaches continuing to be employed long after their usefulness had expired. Having sold a one-time gain as a truly systemic change and needing to keep their shareholders (who had also allocated capital based on those claims) happy, managed care organizations had no other option but to continue squeezing patients and providers harder. The premise by which managed care was sold — that quality can be improved while lowering cost — is, in fact, doable, but *only with sufficient investment in the delivery infrastructure.* Without that investment, the claim becomes an empty, hollow-care promise. No managed care company was more emblematic of this problem than Oxford Health Plans, whose failure to deliver on its promises has been well documented.

What is important to understand is that it does not have to be this way. For example, it is possible to analyze all the steps in the dispensing of a drug and then reengineer the process to lower the dispensing costs and reduce the error rate at the same time. But this means diverting cash flow from shareholders to clinical problem solving. This is a very different approach from the practice used in Hollowcare, which simply eliminates steps in the clinical treatment process to reduce expenditures. Firing the weekend pharmacist at the hospital saves money, but it also can have the impact of *increasing the error rate in the emergency room, especially at 2 o'clock Sunday morning.*

Hollowcare to horror

By and large, managed care organizations have been excellent at talking the talk but have not walked the walk on many needed investments. This is now clearly percolating in the marketplace. The recognition that patients are being squeezed by Hollowcare is contributing to the current backlash from patients, payers, politicians, and the media alike.

Hollowcare gives us horror stories, like the June 15, 1997 cover story in *The New York Times Magazine* that asked, "How Can We Save the Next Victim?" Inside, a lengthy article relates what happened to tiny Jose Eric Martinez, a two-month-old baby in Houston's Hermann Hospital who was given 0.9 milligrams of Digoxin when the prescription called for .09 milligrams to control his heart-failure symptoms. The attending doctor missed the error. No doctor, nurse, pharmacist, or technician corrected it, either. The drug was administered and the infant died soon after.

This blockbuster failure in quality control was just one of the more recent examples. In 1995, Betsy Lehman, 39, ironically a health columnist for *The Boston Globe*, died at Boston's Dana-Farber Cancer Institute from a fourfold miscalculation in the amount of Cytoxan she was being given to cure her breast cancer. That same year, a vascular surgeon at Tampa's University Community Hospital amputated the wrong leg because of a mistake on the surgical schedule. And a surgeon at Memorial Sloan-Kettering Cancer Center in New York operated on the wrong side of a brain because the wrong set of films was brought into the operating room.

Not only has Hollowcare increased the number of tragic human errors, it also has spawned a rise in suspected fraud. U.S.-based Columbia/HCA Healthcare Corporation was the subject of a well-documented massive federal investigation into possible Medicare fraud, a probe that ousted the chief executive officer and key aides. The potential for Medicare fraud has become so huge that the U.S. Federal Bureau of Investigation was recently handling a record 2,300 cases involving mainstream providers.

Meanwhile, dozens of medical centers in the United States are under fire for allegedly padding bills. Columbia/HCA's problems may just be the tip of the iceberg. *The Wall Street Journal* gave front-page treatment to a story about a Columbia hospital in Alabama that charged hundreds of dollars for intravenous fluids administered a day or two after the patient was discharged and for a finger X-ray that was never taken. Home health care companies in at least 10 states are coming under tough scrutiny for purported billing abuses. Other probes focus on hospice operators, community mental health centers, and companies that sell durable medical equipment such as wheelchairs.

Of course, headline-grabbing horror stories and cases of potentially massive fraud have caused an avalanche of proposals for tighter government regulation of managed care. Across the United States, state legislators introduced about 1,000 managed care bills in 1997, including almost 200 that became law. This follows the adoption of 100 such laws in 1996, according to the National Conference of State Legislatures. Recently adopted legislation requires HMOs in a number of states to authorize hospital stays for certain procedures (to prohibit so-called "drive-through mastectomies," for example), to pay for emergency room visits that turn out to have been avoidable, or to allow direct access to obstetricians and certain other specialists without advance permission from a primary care physician. The Patient Bill of Rights that has been proposed in Congress is an example of such issues having reached the Federal level.

While all these efforts are well intentioned, legislators are caught in the trap of trying to practice medicine by statute, a process doomed to failure. Medicine is too complex and fast moving to be effectively run by legislative fiat. If each state goes its own way, the practice of medicine in the United States could become horribly fractured and in so doing, hamstring multi-state employers. Legislators might just as well go home. They would have to vote a hundred new statutes a year to treat all that ails the current health care system. No wonder doctors are selling their practices in record numbers, according to *The Wall Street Journal*.

Patient malaise

The current health care system's problems have not gone unnoticed by patients themselves. There is a serious sense of malaise about the American health system (Table 3.1), according to a recent American Hospital Association survey that includes nearly 24,000 people discharged from some 120 hospitals, along with 13,000 other patients from clinics and doctors' offices, and participants in 12 focus groups. Medical centers are a "nightmare to navigate" for many patients, sending them home before they feel ready and employing uncaring caregivers. From impoverished Medicaid and frail Medicare recipients to individuals with top-of-the-line, employer-sponsored health plans, many expressed angst about reduced access to care, higher expenses and a sense that decisions aren't being made in their best interests.

Table 3.1   Percent of Patients Reporting
Problems

Continuity and transition	28.7%
Emotional support	26.6%
Information and education	23.1%
Involvement of family and friends	22.3%
Coordination of care	22.9%
Respect for patients' preferences	21.8%
Physical comfort	10.4%

Note: Based on a survey of 23,768 patients.

Source: American Hospital Association and the Picker Institute, "Eye on Patients: A Report of the American Public," Pg. 11, 1996.

Based on a their survey, the American Hospital Association and the Picker Institute concluded that there is "an increasing trend toward care that is cold and impersonal." Furthermore, the study concluded that, "the systems put in place to control costs ended up creating barriers to care, especially for people with chronic illnesses." As a result of such an environment, the morale of physicians and medical staff is eroding along with their authority to make medical decisions. Administrative problems have increased. More journals and materials pile up on doctors, who have less time to read them. In fact, doctors in the 1990s likely spend less than half their time in direct contact with patients, with the remaining time divided between either acquiring information or distributing it.

Such, then, is the current state of the medical system, evolved from the twin legacies of past investments in wasteful production capacity, and a current dysfunctional management system. How society moves forward from this position is critical to its future.

chapter four

Opening the Door to Efficientcare

> *The press, the machine, the railway, the telegraph*
> *are premises whose thousand-year conclusion no one*
> *has dared to draw.** *

If medicine is to evolve to serve the needs of the population, it must change its current direction and undergo a revolution. Enabling the revolution in medicine will be the dramatic changes in information technology as expressed by the Internet and e-commerce. These changes will shatter the economic underpinnings of the entire health care delivery system as we know it.

Nowhere will the potential impact be greater than in the epicenter of medical care — the doctor–patient relationship. This, the ground zero of the health care delivery processes, is the location where the revolution begins.

To understand the potential, let us take a closer look at what drives the relationship.

This central processor of health care consists of three elements: acquisition, synthesis, and implementation.

Acquisition

Acquisition is the process by which a patient presents an issue to a doctor or health care provider. The provider's chief objective is to *obtain information*. Why is the patient here? What is the problem? What does the patient want? That information can come in many forms, from an oral history to a physical exam, X-ray or lab test.

---

* Friedrich Nietzsche, in *The Wanderer and His Shadow,* pg. 278, 1880.

The information, once obtained, needs to be stored. The most frequently used and historically least expensive venues for storage included handwritten notes on paper, film, and human memory. Storing the information in the form of electronic bits was historically too expensive and inconvenient. However, the economics of information storage and transmission have undergone a revolution that results in an inversion in the economics of the process. Bits have gone from being the most inconvenient and expensive medium for storage and transmittal to the most efficient.

Synthesis

The second element consists of the provider's *processing and synthesizing* the assembled information database. This database consists of information collected from the patient as well as from other sources such as medical records (charts and films existing prior to the current encounter) and oral communication from other physicians who have relevant information stored in their memories. Journals, publications, and other forms of established, valid medical information are used as supplements.

Only when the information is assembled properly can it be synthesized and processed. Once the stage is set, the doctor can then *think* about the information and combine it with previous experience and knowledge, with the goal of rendering a useful decision or judgment that can be acted upon. The act of rendering judgment and advice represents the bulk of the value-added activity that the doctor or provider is actually trained to perform. Whether influenced by algorithms or managed care constraints, this phase is where clinical resource management decisions are ultimately made.

The ease or difficulty in assembling the information to formulate medical judgments has a direct outcome not only on the quality, but also on the cost of medical treatment. To the extent that the information is incomplete due to missing or lost data, the quality of decisions suffers and the cost rises.

With technology enabling the transfer of information from paper, film, and human memory to electronic bits, the information's use and value improve drastically. Relevant facts no longer get lost. Reliance on faulty human memory decreases. State-of-the-art discoveries are always available. And the costs associated in the movement of the data are drastically reduced. The result is the potential to render a better decision more efficiently and effectively, and at lower costs because the quality of the available database is more accurate, complete, and current.

Implementation

The third element in the patient care process is the *implementation* of decisions based on all available data. Implementation often occurs in the form of a communication or distribution to the patient. The distribution can assume many forms — ordering an additional test to secure more information, writing a prescription, surgical intervention, seeking a change in behavior. The process by which the communication or distribution currently occurs is often cumbersome and may involve duplicating the same information over a dozen times through required insurance forms, medical charts, and preapproval phone calls.

For implementation to be efficacious, it must actually transpire. For example, it is necessary but insufficient for a patient to receive a prescription. The scrip must be filled and the patient must actually take the medicine as instructed before the treatment can be effective. This process of actually following the medical plan is known as compliance. Without compliance, the entire medical service can end up being a total waste of money, time, and effort. For example, one of the biggest wastes of resources involves the annual failure on the part of patients to comply with their medication regimens. Only half of the medicine ordered is actually consumed. Imagine if we only received half of the groceries we paid for at checkout. Yet this happens annually, largely because patients and physicians fail to mutually recognize that they have not come to consensus on their treatment. The result is a huge waste of precious resources.

Failure to comply often results in terrible medical care because the patient ultimately fails to be cured. Paradoxically, very cumbersome, repetitive, wasteful, duplicative, and expensive implementation processes have been created in the name of companies' claiming to be in the business of health and healing, namely managed care. Yet, ironically, as a money-saving measure, they have dramatically increased the likelihood that compliance will not occur. The current inefficient, paper-based, back-seat-driven implementation process virtually guarantees a sub-optimal, unpleasant, and expensive outcome.

In addition, the consequences of failing to comply are growing with the advent of and reliance on treatment algorithms, critical paths, and the like. All of these engineered systems are predicated on the assumption of compliance — that the patient will actually faithfully execute instructions in precise order: first A, then B, then C, etc., time after time. The systems depend on the patients' doing everything they are asked to do. But the real world does not work this way. Patients forget to do what they are asked to do. Patients can be passive–aggressive and look as though they are categorically in agreement when they are not. Patients can be confused. Patients can be scared. Patients can be self-destructive. They can be all of the above. In short, they often act like human beings, but the system that purportedly serves them has been designed assuming that they will behave like automatons.

Reflect on the tragic case of a young female patient who had become pregnant despite using birth control pills. Now trapped in the terrible dilemma of whether to keep the pregnancy, she relayed her frustration that the pills had failed. I spoke to her while I was a third-year medical student. It became clear that she had not understood the simplest elements. Rather than swallow the pills, the patient had understood that they should be inserted vaginally. This human tragedy, which should have been avoided, pointed up the all-too-human, unanticipated consequences of what appeared to be a simple, clear, and foolproof encounter with the health care delivery system.

Treatment regimens can be confusing, complicated, tiring, and painful, even for the most conscientious. If the system assumes compliance where there is none, systems will crash and patient care will deteriorate. Rather than experience the virtuous circle of compliance and cure, patients can end up in a vicious cycle of confusion, failure to get better, and anger over the failure of a system that has every theoretical contingency accounted for except the actual, real-world one.

It is at this very moment, when the treatment fails and the vicious cycle begins, that the intervention of physicians, trained and enabled to provide comfort and understanding, can create the most value. Yet paradoxically, doctors are often hamstrung by protocols and cost pressures that effectively deny them the opportunity to render their maximum value at the time of the most critical need.

Value Chain

If the three elements are linked together as a value chain, then a huge opportunity develops to improve the efficiency and quality of the doctor–patient relationship. We need to seek ways to diminish frictional acquisition and distribution costs and channel most of a provider's time and energy into the second element of the value chain — processing, synthesizing and communicating with patients.

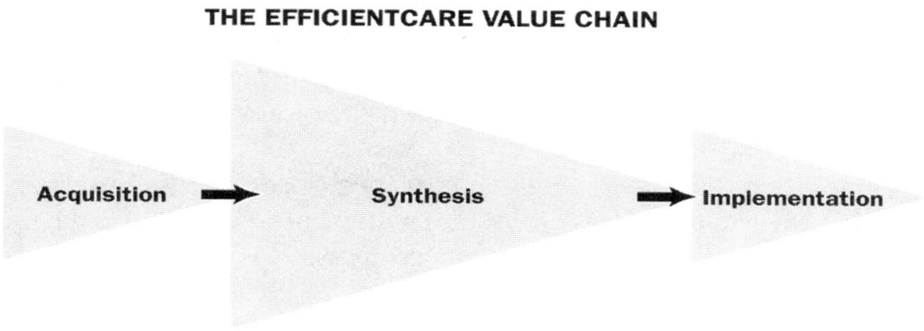

THE EFFICIENTCARE VALUE CHAIN

Acquisition ➡ **Synthesis** ➡ **Implementation**

Figure 4.1

It is within this second element of the value chain that the listening, comforting, talking, soothing, educating, synthesizing — in other words, the art of medicine — really takes place. This value-added phase is where providers exercise good judgment, communicate conclusions, explain treatment options, assist patients in making well-informed decisions and make sure that they are willing and able to comply. Most importantly, this phase is expected to provide *comfort* for patients. It is the art, in combination with the science, of medicine that creates the sense of well-being for patients and contributes to their stock of personal wealth in the form of good health and relief from physical suffering, pain, and disease.

Perversely, however, it is this value-added element of the value chain that is being squeezed from all sides. Increases in medical knowledge combined with more and more onerous utilization controls are compressing the value-added phase by expanding the time and energy needed to acquire and distribute information.

Managed Care compounds the problem

As the physical setting for patient care has migrated out of the hospital to a multitude of locales, the costs associated with moving the necessary information for treatment have increased dramatically, as have the opportunities for misplacing and misinterpreting lab tests, radiographs, medication records, etc. The effort required to assemble and comprehend a complete medical database has become more difficult and expensive than ever before.

This is occurring in spite of the fact that technology is theoretically able to make it easier. The same unfortunate trend in the growth of informational costs has occurred on the distribution end. Actions often cannot happen without cumbersome approval processes designed intentionally to retard the use of resources. Dialing 1-800 "Nurse from Hell" has become all too common for most medical professionals, because they are required to obtain authorization from a managed care company for everything from referrals to hospital admissions.

A vivid example of such events occurred in the Emergency Room at Boston City Hospital when a man came in suicidal. I called 1-800 and the person on the other end said, "We don't want you to admit the patient."

"But I need to," I replied. "He's suicidal."

"How suicidal?" I was asked.

"How suicidal do you want him to be? It's 3 a.m. Well, he has the gun pointed at the floor, so I guess he's not that suicidal. Oops. Sorry, now it's at his temple. Can we admit him now?" I asked.

Sure, it sounds funny, but it was also very real. If I send this person home and he kills himself, I've done a horrible disservice to the patient and probably deserve to lose a malpractice suit. On the other hand, if I admit him to the hospital and his insurance company does not want to pay, I'm bankrupting the hospital. The hospital CEO will call me the next day and yell, "What are you doing here? You're killing me financially."

This kind of back-seat driving ultimately means less time and energy to spend with patients. It also means far more paperwork. With elements one and three of the patient-care process becoming increasingly burdensome, what is discarded is the time for communication between patient and caregiver. This lack of communication is clearly a major contributor to and symptom of Hollowcare.

Parodoxically, the driver of efficiency for the health care delivery engine is element two — information processing. Assume we are wasting nearly 80 percent of total available resources on elements one and three, so the efficiency of the system is roughly 20 percent. Put another way, for any given hour in a doctor's day, 24 minutes is spent on retrieving patient information and another 24 minutes is spent writing prescriptions and pleading with managed care companies to deliver more care. That only leaves 12 minutes to spend with a patient — and people always wonder where their doctors are. While they may assume they're playing golf, on the contrary, they're more likely running around trying to find records or get dispensation. Perhaps this helps explain why the morale of health care professionals is declining. With doctors unable to do the job they were trained for, morale worsens, quality declines, and patients suffer.

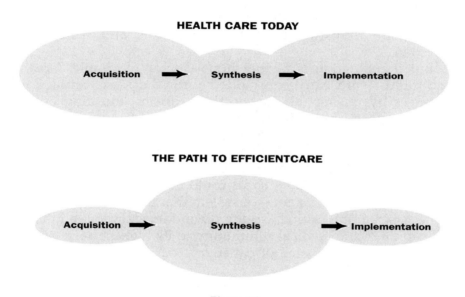

Figure 4.2

A baby dies in Houston because he is accidentally given .9 milligrams instead of .09 milligrams. Had he been at the Brigham and Women's Hospital in Boston, he would probably be alive today. Why? Because that hospital has developed a system that prevents providers from making a dosage error. If doctors want to prescribe morphine, for example, they can do it right from a computer. The computer will request a series of answers to questions such as: How often do you want to give it? Alternately or variably? When would you like to start? How many days? What dosage?

Sadly, rather than using technology to enable and empower, Hollowcare employs it to impede and retard. Put enough anchors on medical professionals and spending will slow down. With

Hollowcare, cost is everything, even if patients stay sicker longer or, tragically, even if they die.

With elements one and three of the process — acquiring information and implementing decisions — ever expanding, element two, the value-added step, is being encroached upon and shrinking. This is the exact opposite of what needs to happen. Given finite resources of intellectual capital, energy, time and money, if society is going to be able to provide the vast amounts of care that elder boomers will require, and not bankrupt the system, the value-added process will need to be *expanded*. The *efficiency* of the engine needs to be *improved*. Rather than sticking to a structural capital component, investment needs to be made and technology deployed.

But the situation is neither hopeless nor inevitable. Greater amounts of care can be provided with the same amount of resources by raising the anchor and reducing the drag on the system imposed by elements one and three. If acquisition and distribution costs could be decreased to 10 percent for each, the number of resources available for element two could increase to 80 percent — a quadrupling of efficiency. In other words, *four times more health care for the same dollar* could be provided with a more efficient health care system — a system that utilizes technology to improve structural capital, freeing up and leveraging the intellectual capital of the medical community to its highest purpose, the care, comfort, and healing of patients.

Becoming digital

How will this revolution occur? When medical information is converted from atoms to bits. When we change the premise by which we deliver care. By shattering the underpinnings of the entire system. By changing the paradigm. By enabling physicians to change their behavior based on the digital revolution. This will dramatically lower the cost of acquiring and distributing information. Then providers can use the information to leverage, not retard, their progress and achieve quantum-leap improvements.

Currently, most medical information resides on paper, film or tape. The fact that the medical record takes a physical form limits the information to being available to one person at one place and at one time. Such a simple but fundamental constraint on information has, until recently, underpinned both the economics and the organization of the current medical delivery system.

Because medical records aren't mobile, the medical system traditionally moved the *patient*, rather than the *information*, from location to location. To get treatment, a patient had to physically visit a hospital or a doctor's office where the information was stored. If the patient lived in an area not convenient to a medical facility, he or she traveled or did without care. This quaint and inefficient concept of moving the patient, not the information, is rapidly becoming so obsolete as to be intolerable. What will take its place will transform the delivery platform.

To gain perspective, let us recall the Lewis and Clark expedition of 1804. As Meriwether Lewis and his company attempted to traverse the western United States, as chronicled in *Undaunted Courage*, they were able to physically move people and goods no faster than the Romans could 2,000 years before. Why? Because Lewis undertook his trip before the availability of the steam engine, or locomotive. As a result, the trip was arduous, and the likelihood of settling the West by more than a few hale and hardy men seemed unlikely. However, once the steam engine was invented and the railroads were built by the mid-1800s, mankind's ability to move about physically was radically transformed. The concept of insurmountable distance was changed forever, radically altering the ability of the young United States to populate the continent. Frontiers began to disappear. The dream of manifest destiny became a practical reality.

In the same way, until recently, mankind's ability to move information has been no better than Caesar's. Information either was memorized or inscribed on paper or film (or a stone tablet, in the case of the Romans) and moved from place to place as needed. The physical format severely constrained the ability to process information simultaneously, in parallel with other humans. While the subsequent printing press and today's photocopy machines helped, the physical settings in which information could be exchanged were still limited, especially when that information was dynamic and constantly changing. The paper containing the information had to reside in a fixed location or library. The only way to gain access to it was to present oneself in person to the arena where that information was stored. In fact, the need to store medical information helped stimulate the construction of the modern hospital, much the same way that the advent of writing encouraged the Greeks to first build libraries.

But, in the blink of an eye, electronic bits change everything. They convert information from atoms of paper or film to bits of digital communication that can be transmitted anywhere, anytime, at blinding speed. Now medical information can move at the velocity of light and be disseminated to multiple users at the same time at a low marginal cost. No longer must patients move to the information. Information can be brought to them, in the city or in the country, at sea or in the air. Providers and patients are no longer bound by physical constraints to provide and receive treatment. Care giving becomes possible at an unlimited number of locations. Medical care can be imported and exported globally. The traditional concept of hospitals and doctors becomes no longer competitively valid. The entire economics of medical care is shattered and changed forever. The invisible hand of the marketplace can be liberated to move and rearrange the system and reward investment in structural and intellectual capital.

With the elimination of economic and physical constraints on the movement of medical information, the art of the possible dramatically expands. A vastly more efficient and satisfying health care system becomes a possibility, although not a certainty. Necessary but insufficient conditions are created to allow the construction of a health care system that is desperately needed, given the looming elder-boomer demands for greater care.

In much the same way that few could imagine, as Meriwether Lewis was struggling up the Missouri River in the early 1800s, that it would be possible within a few short decades for hundreds of thousands of people to rush off to the West and look for gold, the health care system is poised to undergo a revolution. The capitalist marketplace today, in its never-ending quest for the next gold field, always looking for a cheaper, faster, and better way to provide care, is poised to finance it. And entrepreneurs, enabled with the vision, are poised to build it.

chapter five

The Virtual Health Care System

*The system is virtual. The care is real.**

Enabled by technology and best-of-breed resources, the next revolution in health care will be "HealthCare.com." HealthCare.com can close the book on Hollowcare and lead providers and patients alike into a lasting era of Efficientcare — a time when health care is redesigned from the inside out to deliver not just higher quality at lower costs but maximum value as well.

In my proposed vision of the future, there will be a Virtual Health Care System representing a network of providers united by technology and contractual relationships rather than by common ownership or control. Each provider will be chosen for what it does best — cancer treatment, say, or pediatrics. Information systems will allow providers to change behavior and link themselves together in a web-like delivery system. The net effect will be the equivalent of medical all-star teams.

Structural capital deployed in the form of virtual health care networks has the potential to break down walls that segregate providers and free them to deliver best-of-class value in their area of specialty. Virtual health care delivery systems will leverage both intellectual and financial capital more efficiently. Expertise can be shared and rented, not owned. Interaction among the components can take multiple forms, including partnerships, alliances, contracts, and ownership. The entire clinical process can be managed

* *Extended Clinical Consulting by Hospital Computer Networks*, Donald F. Parsons, Carl M. Fleisher, and Robert A. Greenes (Eds.), New York Academy of Sciences, New York, 1992.

as a synthetic singular clinical system with best-of-class components, accessed by providers on behalf of patients.

Once the expertise is in place, all the pieces can be linked by technology for efficient information transfer. Clinical and financial information can be made available through video, audio, and text links. Systems can be streamlined and duplicated functions removed to generate tremendous efficiencies. Behavior can be modified, the rules of the game changed, red tape eliminated and value maximized. In the United States alone, virtual systems have the potential to dramatically reduce a significant percentage of the nation's $1 trillion health care price tag, not only by replacing time-consuming, structurally inefficient capital with superior information gathering and distribution capabilities, but also by improving patient treatment and compliance.

The core concept: virtual webs

Virtual health care systems are based on changing the nature of structural capital to virtual webs of providers linked together through technology and contractual relationships to provide specific goods or services. Webs supply all needed services, including surgery, intensive care, rehabilitation, pharmaceuticals, home health care, and durable medical equipment. If hospitals can be compared to department stores, webs are analogous to shopping malls, where a variety of boutiques provide wider selection and better service more efficiently. In a virtual health care world, hospitals will become more like shopping malls as their services are unbundled and repositioned as webs.

Virtual health care webs force providers to focus on their areas of excellence and to invest in areas where they can generate a sustainable competitive advantage. Webs also provide opportunities to break bottlenecks by allowing for multiple suppliers. Instead of forcing patients to wait in line to get an X-ray from the only local radiologist, a web might use teleradiology to allow multiple radiologists from hundreds or even thousands of miles away to read X-rays, thereby increasing the throughput of the system. Ultimately, webs can link providers to enable delivery of higher-quality care at a lower price than is currently possible with integrated hospitals that try to be all things to all people. The upside is potentially much greater value for the health care dollar.

With webs, communities can be created that allow medical intellectual capital to become amassed and concentrated in order to be applied to clinical problems. The key social activity in medicine — learning, which traditionally has occurred in groups at the bedside — can be leveraged logarithmically through virtual medical communities. Patients can now receive not only the best their own doctor has to offer, but the best from a team of doctors. Because the costs of creating, manipulating, and transporting information electronically is so much cheaper than before, patients can receive the coordinated benefits and leverage from a team of many minds for the market price of one.

Medical communities or webs are not owned, but rather controlled, by providers known as "shapers," the Microsofts of the world, that have enough clout to set prevailing treatment patterns. Other providers, known as "adapters," support the webs and provide the services required, much as Intuit supports Microsoft by leading the niche market for financial software.

To expand on the web analogy for a moment, Microsoft created a web in the computer industry. Its operating system functions as an enabler to the industry, but the company today captures only about 4 percent of the total value in the computer marketplace. It works with key suppliers, like Intel, the chip maker, that it treats as partners. Microsoft does not own Intel and Intel does not own Microsoft, but they work together to build a Wintel operating environment that allows the leveraging of each other's intellectual and financial capital more effectively than either could do by itself. In a web-based community, participants offer distinctive value, like the software companies whose applications work with Microsoft operating systems and Intel chips. There are many participants, each focusing on a specific niche. And there are multiple suppliers, just as there are many computer makers.

In contrast, health care systems that avoid a web approach and attempt to control everything, similar in strategy to Apple Computer, which tried to do everything in the late 1980s, are likely to falter. This failure to understand webs is one of the key reasons so many integrated delivery systems also are doomed.

Most medical-provider mergers will ultimately waver because they still hark back to the Wastecare model of integrated service delivery, which in and of itself is both inefficient and expensive. The situation is akin to sinking ships lashing themselves together and hoping they will float. Or, to use another analogy, taking two engines that get one mile per gallon and gluing them together in the vain hope of getting 10 miles per gallon. With the structural capital flawed, the likelihood of success is unacceptably low.

Hopefully, virtual systems will begin to emerge from the wreckage of managed care. As investors become disillusioned with current models and the need to reinvent the wheel intensifies, the seeds of the virtual system will grow. Columbia/HCA, which had bought home heath care concerns and pharmacy operations in addition to hospitals before its legal troubles, could provide an excellent platform. It has begun to reorganize into eight "product lines": cancer, cardiology, diabetes, behavioral health, workers' compensation, women's services, senior care and emergency services. But only time will tell if they can successfully migrate to a new model.

How webs work

One vision of Virtual health care systems consists of three different webs:

1. Preventive
2. Treatment
3. Chronic

A Preventive Web™ (Figure 5.1) focuses on maintaining and enhancing the overall health of the population, emphasizing preventive care, screening, and education in order to prevent illness from manifesting itself in ways that are expensive and harmful to patients. Preventive Webs are now being developed for cholesterol and weight reduction, heart attack prevention, and the management of hypertension, diabetes, and osteoporosis.

As we envision it, an elderly woman at risk for osteoporosis would be treated in a Preventive Web, where her doctor would encourage exercise and a calcium-rich diet. If, despite these best efforts, she falls and breaks her hip, her doctor would direct her to a Treatment Web (Figure 5.2). A Treatment Web would provide her with emergency assistance at a critical care center, as well as rehabilitation, home health care, and durable medical equipment services.

For chronic conditions, such as diabetes, she would be directed to a Chronic Care Web™ (Figure 5.3) for the appropriate medication, education and monitoring.

Web-based care has the potential to change the way disease is managed and the way physicians behave in their practice of medicine. Currently, there is little agreement on the best way to treat

Figure 5.1 Preventive Web. (Source: Watson Wyatt Worldwide, 1999.)

Figure 5.2 Treatment Web. (Source: Watson Wyatt Worldwide, 1999.)

illnesses. Clinical protocols, for the most part, are art forms founded on local beliefs. Take something as simple as dressing a wound. Some surgeons first apply wet dressings, then a dry one, but others say no, put a dry one on first and then a wet one.

Most doctors were trained to treat patients based on the particular belief system of their senior colleagues. But on what science was this based? Reflecting on my own training, much of what we

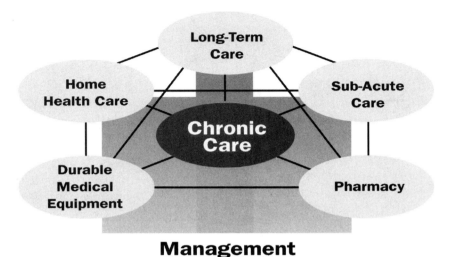

Management

Figure 5.3   Chronic Care Web. (Source: Watson Wyatt Worldwide, 1999.)

were taught was tradition masquerading as fact. It got to the point where when I walked into a new hospital as a medical student, I would always be on the lookout for their local belief system. This needs to change. Outcome-driven data is the only rational future. Show doctors — and prove it on a global basis — that if they do provide treatment, they will get outcome. Demonstrate a standard of care that is the best in the world and communicate it through the Internet so that it becomes the new gold standard, replacing locally based rules that rely on tradition for their legitimacy.

This will happen when medicine focuses on global best practices — removing mindless algorithms that assume patients are robots and replacing them with real-world, real-time best thinking through access to vast amounts of information on past and current patients, including treatments and outcomes. The Internet can help immensely by tracking and providing data on what works and what doesn't, who complies and who doesn't, and what can be done to fix it. With virtual systems and worldwide information links, information can be readily available. Physicians and other health care professionals can punch in specifics about a patient's symptoms, health history, and numerous other variables and get back a treatment plan for everything from length of hospital stay to drug regimen and exercise recommendations.

Akin to what Rosabeth Moss Kanter at the Harvard Business School calls "mass customization," this approach can combine the best of both worlds — in-depth knowledge about individual patients and widespread knowledge about possible courses of treatment. But health care delivery is still custom work. It offers opportunities to provide and create special relationships that enhance the patient's experience. This is where the old-fashioned doctor–patient relationship can reemerge refreshed, updated, and more valuable and satisfying than ever.

At the same time, protocols can finally be used productively. Demand management protocols in a Preventive Web, for example, can be designed to help prevent illness (Figure 5.4). Disease management protocols in a Chronic Care Web can specify the best way to treat illnesses such as asthma. Episode management protocols in a Treatment Web can stipulate best practices for treating a broken leg. Aside from the obvious comfort afforded to patients from knowing that they are receiving the best treatment possible, based on thousands if not millions of similar cases, such a method will improve medical practice around the world. Whether an appendix ruptures in India or Iowa, patients will have a far better chance of getting the same excellent treatment based on the best current thinking the world of medicine has to offer.

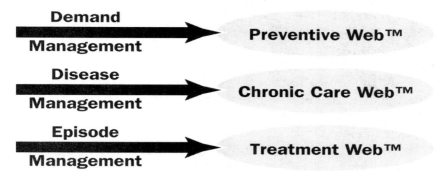

Figure 5.4 Virtual Health Care System™. (Source: Watson Wyatt Worldwide, 1999.)

Not all parties will be happy with this revolution. Those entities currently profiting from the collective inefficiency of the system will find their very economic existence threatened. One clear example of the potential threat is in the area of disease management. A drug company might desperately want to get into the disease-management business to ensure that doctors prescribe its product. But what happens if the best practice excludes its product? What happens if its product is unneeded? These producers have a powerful incentive either to derail or hijack the process. Such behavior would not be unexpected and is, in fact, consistent with a free market. The key to keeping the medical market for ideas working at optimum levels will be to create conditions guaranteeing that ideas are constantly pressure-tested against each other. The more open the market, the more widely disseminated the information becomes. The more sunshine let into the process, the better the end result.

Linking it all together

Just as global information will be critical for implementing standardized treatment protocols, global information technology will be the glue that binds webs, providers, and patients together into communities. No longer will the doctor or the patient be moved to the information. Separate and far-flung computer systems can be integrated so health care professionals can retrieve all of a patient's records whenever and wherever necessary.

When vital information becomes easy to access, doctors will spend more time thinking, processing, and interacting with patients. Treatment will become more efficient. Quality control will improve markedly when hard copies of patient files are converted into electronic form. Medical orders that once were illegible will now be clear. X-rays that were missing or medical records that were inaccessible can now be available instantly. Discharge, diagnostic, and operative notes will be able to contain qualitative and contextual content, such as video clips of the patients' physical and emotional reaction to their clinical situations and their interactions with their healers.

The privacy of this information should actually be improved from the current sieves that are used to control paper. Technology that permits the secure transmission of spy-satellite photography can help make the system far more secure than its current paper-based format. Nonetheless, the issue of privacy will be a huge issue that will need to be addressed constantly.

Globally linked databases will make it easier to find a doctor who can maximize the relationship with the patient. All the details of doctors' degrees, residencies, fellowships, clinical interests, and languages, along with video clips of physicians describing their clinical interests and experience, treatment philosophy, interpersonal style, and other "soft" information can be available. Need a specialist who speaks Chinese and has written articles on breast cancer treatment? No problem. Here are the articles and a video clip of the doctor discussing treatment options. This kind of system will give patients a level of comfort they can't get by paging through a directory of physicians' names and addresses.

The personal touch — anywhere in the world

Backed by the power of technology, Virtual health care systems will allow providers to redefine their markets and cover a greater geographic area. Local, state, and national barriers to entry will dissolve over time. New therapies will spread faster as local standards of care and other barriers to good treatment become obsolete.

Yet the personal touch should not only remain but become enhanced. Patients will still have contact with their doctors — in fact, thanks to technology, they should have greater access than ever before. And doctors, freed from the tyranny of information retrieval and distribution impediments, should actually have more time to spend caring for their patients.

chapter six

Changing Roles

Call me self-righteous or harebrained or a windbag.
*Just don't call me a provider.**

The biggest barrier to implementing Efficientcare will not be the technology. As futuristic as it sounds, for the most part it exists today. It will not be money, because that will become available as the size of the opportunity becomes clearer. The biggest barrier will be changing physician behavior and the way the health care system deploys its collective intellectual capital.

At its core, the most critical element of health care is intellectual capital. Bricks and mortar never took care of anyone at 2 a.m. A better understanding of how to leverage technology, finance, and management competencies to help shape the deployment of intellectual capital is essential if health care is to be delivered through virtual systems that operate at efficient and full potential.

Technology alone cannot replace doctors. Patients will not be cared for by robots. Managed properly, technology should serve as a great enabler. As a viable tool, however, it will be incumbent upon managers within the system to learn, understand, and master it. The installation of an advanced technology-based delivery platform will require managers skilled in capital allocation and leverage. Compensation arrangements that reflect new performance-based measurements and criteria will need to evolve. People and project management skills will compose the critical competencies organizations will require to manage the new interlocking relationships and changing roles that all the involved parties will face.

---

* Richard Fleming, MD, in "A physician's lament: Call me doc, call me self-righteous or call me a windbag," *Newsweek*, June 9, 1997, pg. 20.

Effectively redefining the role and uses of intellectual capital will be the key to making the new strategies work. Providers will need to migrate from non-cost-conscious, collegial environments to more competitive, yet collaborative, situations. Referrals will need to be made on the basis of value, cost, and quality, not because of the referring physician's personal relationships with the specialist. Organizational design will need to align provider incentives to attain the highest levels of quality while maximizing value received. Medicine will no longer be able to run as a provincial enterprise. The cottage industry is over. The provider steeped in 13th-century management practices will need to leap forward to the next millennium in order to survive.

More-accountable patients

During the next 10 years, every player in health care delivery will take on a new role (Figure 6.1). To paint the picture more clearly, let's start with the patients, on whom the whole system should be focused.

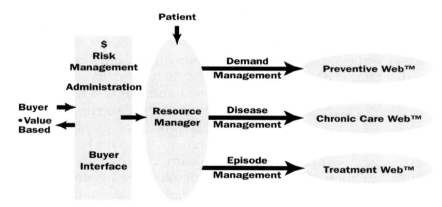

Figure 6.1   Virtual Health Care System. (Source: Watson Wyatt Worldwide, 1999.)

Instead of just showing up at a doctor's office and passively seeking treatment, patients will be expected to be more accountable for their health status and to act as partners in their treatment. In short, they'll have to become better-educated health care consumers. They will be expected to take more responsibility for what happens to them. Who's expecting this? Their employers, to begin with, who need them to stay healthy, be at work, functioning at peak performance, and adding maximum value at their jobs through their own human capital. Employees will be expected to help hold down costs at the workplace and contribute to their company's financial performance. Healthy employees will become a competitive corporate advantage.

As the employers who pay the bills continue to exert pressure on the medical system to become more efficient, doctors also can expect to find their patients accountable and wishing to become partners in prevention to ensure that valuable resources are not wasted. Employers will want their employees to understand that they, the patients themselves, will increasingly bear the brunt of the cost of treatment for diseases that are avoidable due to smoking, poor nutrition, or failure to take medicines or wear seat belts. Those patients who choose to engage in risky behavior or fail to exercise will increasingly be held accountable for the medical consequences.

For instance, current best medical practice for males over age 40 with family histories of heart attacks is to take an aspirin a day to reduce the chances of a heart attack. In the future, during their annual physical exam, they will be asked about aspirin intake and compliance, as well as weight and eating habits. The ratio of body fat to lean muscle mass will be examined as well as their exercise regime. Prevention will be uppermost in mind, if only because the heart attack that never happens will always be a better and cheaper outcome than the one that does.

From physician to "resource manager"

Physicians will be expected to become more accountable too, moving from being self-centered to patient-centered. If Dr. Fleming doesn't like being called a "provider" now, imagine how he's going to feel when he's called a "resource manager." But that's just what he'll be, responsible for allocating health care resources and directing patients to the most appropriate webs. All the while, his task will be to minimize resources utilized and maximize patient outcomes. In short, he will become a "value maximizer." Ultimately, resource managers will be held accountable and compensated on the basis of how well they handle their patients and create value. Even a health index that measures the total value added to the health of the patient population could be used to evaluate the performance of health care practitioners responsible for managing care.

From provider to fiduciary

The mission of providers will be to care for their population on a continuous basis, improving the quality or health indices of the population over time. In essence, they will become not just the patient's physician but the patient's advocate, vested with a nearly fiduciary obligation to the patient's health. They will be responsible for finding the best, cheapest, quickest, fastest, highest-quality treatment components available. When a superior treatment is developed, the resource manager will be expected to eliminate the inefficient component and introduce the new one. In sum, a resource manager will be in charge of making sure patients and buyers alike get maximum health and value for their dollar.

This represents a very significant cultural change. As employers and patients become more active in changing health care, the medical profession will have to shift its focus. Credentials will be paired with competencies to determine a physician's capabilities. Where doctors did their residencies will be less important than what they can do. Competition to be the best will intensify because information will be easier to obtain. In a world where an X-ray filmed in Boston can be read in Baltimore, everyone becomes a competitor and the concepts of best available local care lose their meaning.

Unknowing to all-knowing patients

Thanks to the Internet, patients today have more access to information than ever before. The entire contents of the Library of Congress can fit on their kitchen table. The typical profile of an Internet surfer is a 38-year-old female looking up health information for someone in her immediate family. If she wants to understand treatment options for multiple sclerosis, she might enter an electronic chat room, where she might learn that there are at least 12 different drugs being tried in six different studies and countries. After cruising the 'Net, she is likely to show up in a medical office and say, "OK, doctor, here are all the printouts. What do you think about all this? What is the best treatment? What medicine should I take?" My first thought, as her doctor, is that I have no clue, because for the first time in the history of medicine she has more information than I do. It was not supposed to be this way.

Like all doctors, I was taught in medical school to memorize information, regurgitate it and be prescriptive. The name of the game was to memorize. He who memorized the most won. My old role model was the great and powerful Wizard of Oz — the Oz who knew more than the patients and dispensed wisdom and information with aplomb. But that won't work anymore. Now doctors will have to help patients acquire the information, filter out the junk from the truth, and process and synthesize the information in order to reach a conclusion so the patient and doctor can become partners.

This represents a huge fundamental change in the basic patient–doctor relationship. In the old system of Hollowcare, doctors were gatekeepers. Their job was to keep patients away from medical care because they had been transformed into closet rationers. Like gas station attendants during the 1970s oil shortages, they were told to tell patients, sorry, no gas today, come back tomorrow. But in the future, doctors will help patients access the system, manage the process and optimize resource use. Frankly, that is a much more fulfilling job. The more information patients have, the more they can participate in their care. If doctors are going to be paid as resource managers, they won't want patients who are professional victims. That behavior will destroy their bottom lines. They will want patients who will also take responsibility for getting well.

Rethinking medical education

What does this mean for doctors-to-be? It means a total rethinking of the skills they will need to function effectively in the future. Most medical schools today still train doctors based on outdated precepts. With one foot in the 20th century and the other in the 13th, medical schools are acting as impediments to change rather than leading the charge. As a consequence, advances in medical delivery are coming from everywhere except organized medicine — consulting firms, pharmaceutical companies, MCOs, and HMOs. However, none of these institutions are truly independent; they all have a vested interest in manipulating the outcome. The medical schools — the truly objective and potentially most capable source, where innovation should evolve — are nowhere to be found. If the schools are to avoid mass closings and flourish again, they need to get both feet into the new millennium.

"Bit map" medicine

Information, communication, and technology are shattering the underpinnings of the conventional practice of medicine. The doctor who memorizes the most information is no longer the best. There's just too much information and the amount doubles every two years, much of it just plain wrong. Five thousand scientific articles were printed last year. How many can be memorized by one individual doctor — or even read, let alone be turned into useful action that creates value for patients?

Since medicine is a learning-based profession, we must teach how to learn again. To again quote Thomas Stewart in *Intellectual Capital*, "We need to increase the structural capital of the profession in order to bank lessons learned. Without a culture of teamwork and the compensation and rewards to support it, the garden of knowledge will be as forlorn as a playground built next to a senior-only condo." Medical schools need to teach physicians and nurses how to manage resources and how to access the system. Schools need to invent new cultures, recognition, and reward systems in addition to making discoveries in molecular biology and pharmaceuticals.

Society needs to rethink the competencies they want doctors to possess and rethink what their training should consist of. Ironically, the most valuable lessons learned in medical school may be to look into a patient's eyes, and ask, "What do you think is wrong with you?" then listen attentively to their concerns. More often than not, patients know what is wrong with them. People need to participate in their care and treatment in order for it to be effective. Medical education should teach doctors how to let them do so.

In the United States, medical training consists of four expensive years of college followed by four expensive years of medical school — all of which students pay for themselves — plus three or more years of residency, where they are being paid at below-market rates. Essentially, in order to become a trained doctor in the U.S., we ask people to sacrifice 12 years of their lives and finally emerge at age 30 with about $200,000 of debt.

Does medical care really require 12 years of post-high-school training to do 80 percent of the tasks performed? Most of the rest of the world mints doctors four to five years post-high school. In an era of resource constraint, these issues need to be aired and debated. Thankfully, they have begun to receive closer scrutiny. In a series of reports beginning in 1992, the Pew Health Professions

Commission recommended a variety of changes in medical education. Suggestions include closing 20 percent of U.S. medical schools and cutting back on the training of new doctors, nurses, and pharmacists. The idea is to match medical education to the needs of the "emerging health system" of the 21st century. For instance, the commission recommended modifying or ending the 13th-century practice of tenure, by which medical schools are obligated to keep all their faculty members until retirement, regardless of their performance.

Ultimately, society must ask what it wants. It can spend $40 per person per year on health care, as Gambia does; $400, as China does; or $4,000, as the United States does. Years ago, American society decided that it wanted very well-educated, well-rounded people to make medical decisions. Now it is saying it wants low-cost service providers. Can society make do with less-trained individuals? Will it be getting something different? Will it be paying for steak and receiving Spam instead? What exactly does society want from its medical intellectual capital? How much of our national human capital and wealth do we want to expend on health care? How well trained do you want the person taking care of you to be when you're having chest pain at 2 a.m.?

New roles for insurers and HMOs

Insurance companies and HMOs will face a sea change as well. Currently, they play three roles: They are marketers, sending glossy brochures and boasting about the number of lives they cover; distributors, signing up as many health care professionals as possible; and they are claim payers.

All of these roles will change, as buyers increasingly go directly to suppliers and cut out the middleman to save money. If insurers and HMOs are to survive, they will need to acquire three additional core competencies.

First, they will need to redefine their relationship with customers — from one of marketing, where they apply the dictum of *caveat emptor*, to a fiduciary relationship where they accept the duty to do what's best for the patient. If they do not evolve in this direction on their own accord, it is likely that they will be compelled legislatively. The State of Texas recently passed a law allowing patients to sue HMOs for malpractice, clearly setting the stage for the coming debate on the issue of fiduciary responsibility.

Second, rather than simply distributing whatever is available, insurers and managed care companies will need to become filters and consolidators, selecting the best providers and treatment modalities to the exclusion of poor performers. This role will require substantial expenditures for monitoring clinical data and tracking outcomes.

Third, instead of just paying claims, they will need to function as capital and technology suppliers to the health care industry. They will have to provide sophisticated risk management services. They will need to create a buyer interface that plugs members into the virtual health care model and sets the delivery process into motion. To create a more effective relationship between the buyers and the health care resources, managed care companies will need to handle a huge array of information on quality and outcomes, as well as integrate clinical data, handle claims transactions efficiently and market their services effectively. With their access to the capital markets and business management, they are well positioned to do so. But they and their investors have to be willing to reinvent themselves.

Profound consequences

If they insist on functioning under the old model, HMOs likely face slow extinction because of the ability of the market to bypass them through direct contracting on the part of buyers and resource managers. Buyers are demanding greater accountability and value for dollars spent. HMOs have been criticized for diverting a significant amount of cash away from clinical care. The medical loss ratio in the United States (a measure of how much money was spent on direct medical care) was as low as 69 cents on the dollar in the mid-1990s. Of the remaining 31 cents of every premium dollar, 11 cents was spent on salaries and general and administrative expenses, while 20 cents went to shareholders as dividends and earnings.

To more and more health care buyers, this smells of skimming. No longer entirely satisfied by the general contractor for their health care "house," buyers are beginning to scrutinize the subcontractors and contemplate direct buys. For their part, subcontractors, like hospitals and physician groups, are approaching buyers directly as well, offering to take on the general contractor role and belittling HMOs as mere administrators.

In essence, everyone is competing to become the general contractor because that's where the money is. Fully 20 percent of the U.S. gross domestic product is up for grabs, and the consequences are profound. Information management can and will redefine entire markets. Oxford Health Plans has been a major force in New York City, but with its recent problems, it is vulnerable to competition. Minnesota's Mayo Clinic has penetrated Arizona, and the Cleveland Clinic has a foothold in Florida.

Why stop at state or national borders? Why not go around the world? Disease is disease, whether you're Chinese, Russian, or American. Barriers to entry are evaporating. Eventually, geographic constraints on physician licensing will, too. Yesterday's constraints to success were the number of available beds, the location of medical records, and access to and contractual relationships with, local doctors. Tomorrow's competitive advantages will come from a mastery of technology, finance, and management.

Suppliers will evolve as multiple local standards of care give way to an ever-demanding global standard of care. Right now, patients living in out-of-the-way locales are limited to what is locally available in the care they can receive. In the future, they will demand the best care available on earth, as Boris Yeltsin did when he needed heart bypass surgery, and received it in Moscow from a Houston-based medical team.

Two choices

Just as pop culture mirrors the values of each country, so do health care systems. Subsidized socialist systems in Europe, Canada, and Asia are no longer working well. Managed care is not the answer in the United States. Societies the world over are facing two fundamental choices: Ration care, which is akin to rationing gas, as we did during the worldwide oil shortage 25 years ago, or build a more fuel-efficient car.

Simply spending less money per person does not mean that a system is more efficient. The car may just be traveling a shorter distance, not getting more miles per gallon. The future of health care lies in actually constructing a more fuel- or information-efficient engine. Though this endeavor may create near-term dislocations and require considerable adjustments, the resulting Efficientcare will be far preferable to the painful choices that lie in wait for our parents, our children, and ourselves if we fail to act and continue on the road to Hollowcare.

chapter seven

Paying Hippocrates*

*Never do harm to anyone.***

If a more efficient system is to be built, the financial incentives driving the medical system's intellectual capital will need to change. If we want physicians and managed care organizations to focus on increasing miles per gallon rather than just resorting to rationing, we will need to totally rethink what behavior we want and how to encourage it.

As traditional fee-for-service medicine is replaced with capitated arrangements, the potential exists for creating incentives that contradict the legal, moral, and ethical imperatives of patient care. Capitation arrangements evolved to solve the problems of excessive testing, examinations, X-rays, etc. While some of these excesses may have been a result of medicine's defensiveness against malpractice litigation, doctors also gained economically from traditional fee-for-service medicine with little or no real utilization controls. However, as the United States begins to adopt capitation as the predominant form of compensation, we need to ask whether the pendulum has swung too far from focusing on patient care to obsessing over cost savings.

As an example, consider the following hypothetical situation. A primary care physician who is receiving full capitation for all patient services, tests, and professional fees receives a phone call at 2 a.m. from a patient who is having chest pain.

---

* This chapter is excerpted from an article by the same title that first appeared in 1996 in *Physician Compensation*. Also contributing to the article were three of my Watson Wyatt colleagues: Ira T. Kay, Ph.D., Global Practice Director, Executive Compensation; Jamie S. Hale, C.C.P., C.E.B.S., Practice Director for Strategic Rewards; and Heidi J. Töppel, C.P.A., Executive Compensation Practice Leader in the east region United States.
** Hippocratic Oath, Oxford University Press, London, New York, 1974.

Under the old fee-for-service system, there was no doubt that the patient would be asked to go to the emergency room for evaluation by an ER physician and/or the patient's private primary care doctor. During the visit, a determination would be made as to the patient's state of health (whether in fact it was a heart attack), the need for both urgent and chronic treatment of the chest pain, and consideration for possible admission and additional tests.

In this example, the physician understood that his or her primary imperative was to the patient, period. Financial compensation was irrelevant because it was understood that he or she would receive a fee for waking up, getting out of bed, going down to the hospital, and taking care of the patient in the middle of the night. Even if that patient only had gastritis (an upset stomach) as opposed to a heart attack, the physician was secure in the knowledge that he or she would be paid. Further, it had been drilled into the doctor through a decade or more of training that the physician's Hippocratic obligation was to provide all the care that the patient needed, without limitation or regard to personal financial consideration.

In the new world of capitation, however, the potential for competing fiduciary, contractual, and compensation interests and incentives can have discomforting implications.

Through the lens of capitation, let's reexamine that 2 a.m. phone call. Imagine now that when the patient calls the physician, the physician decides to tell the patient to simply ignore the pain, go back to bed, and call back the next morning if the pain persists. If the patient suffers a massive heart attack and dies in bed, a wonderful — though perverse — thing happens from an actuarial and cost point of view:

- The physician does not have to get out of bed and go to the hospital.
- The physician does not have to incur an ER charge to the capitation risk pool.
- The physician does not have to risk the potential cost of hospitalizing the patient in an intensive care unit or subjecting the patient to expensive emergency coronary artery bypass surgery or cardiac catheterization procedures that would further drain tens of thousands of dollars from the financial risk pool.

From the point of view of the health plan's finances, then, the patient's death represents a positive actuarial event. Imagine how pleased most employees would be to announce to their employers that they had saved the firm more than $100,000 with just one decision made the night before.

However wonderful this outcome may be for the shareholders of the health plan, and for the physician's income, it clearly is not wonderful for the patient.

To further compound the problem, imagine that the physician, despite the financial interest to not do so, gets out of bed and admits the patient to the hospital to rule out a heart attack, only to find that the pain is simple heartburn. Two days later, the physician has to explain to his or her employer that $5,000 had been wasted trying to treat heartburn at the telemetry care unit. Imagine how unhappy an employer would be to hear an employee had just wasted $5,000.

Though clearly fictional and not truly reflective of compensation arrangements, this story drives home the point that compensation matters.

While many non-monetary factors motivate physicians — the desire for healthy patients, a love of science — the economic incentives dangled in front of doctors should not directly conflict with their moral, ethical and legal duties to treat patients.

One way to balance the Hippocratic imperative with the need to save money is to design compensation systems that rationally balance the competing interests of patients, doctors, and health plan shareholders. Unfortunately, however, this area has received far less attention than it deserves.

Many capitated reimbursement schemes are being introduced without careful study and without clear consideration of their potential consequences. The most devastating consequence is reduced morale among physicians, stemming directly from a contradictory compensation system that financially induces doctors to provide minimal amounts of care in violation of moral, ethical, and legal imperatives drilled into them from the start of medical school.

In response to these concerns, the contracting parties say "not to worry" because doctors will do the right thing for the patient, regardless of the compensation scheme. But this is a myth. Watson Wyatt's work in the executive compensation arena shows that economic incentives must support the proper behaviors, not impede them.

The financial challenge

Under a capitated system, physicians receive a flat payment for each patient to whom they are assigned. That payment can be limited to physician services only, or it can be expanded broadly to include additional services such as hospitalizations and diagnostic tests. The payment can be to an individual physician or, more commonly, to a physician group. This change from fee-for-service compensation has had a powerful result. Under the old system, the physician's only risks were providing bad care with poor outcomes for the patient and tort liability. As a result, physicians were motivated to order tests and services, per their training, in sufficient quantity to ensure the best possible outcome for the patient, regardless of cost. Of course, receiving fees for each service also made such practice quite lucrative. It is no wonder this environment is often referred to by doctors as the "golden age" of medicine.

Under the new system of capitation, both the tort issue and the moral, ethical, and legal duties to provide excellent patient care still remain. Now, however, physicians are caught in a squeeze between those forces and a financial system that severely limits the resources at their command. Therefore, physicians are increasingly being forced to choose between the cost of care and the health outcomes of patients. When physicians themselves have an economic stake in providing less medicine, it may be impossible for doctors to perform rationally.

This problem is compounded by a lack of good outcome research indicating what types of care are the most valuable and cost-effective. Sadly, conflicting claims abound about the efficacy of treatment options, providing a poor compass for doctors trying to navigate through this maze.

The dilemma for physicians is that they are compelled financially to make appropriate choices without good information on the outcomes of those choices. In the past, this was never an issue because medicine simply assumed the more tests, the better; the longer the hospital stay, the better. But now the paradigm is changing.

In the absence of reliable data, physicians will be tempted to use the low-cost option. This will occur not because of moral, ethical, and legal imperatives but rather because, in the absence of a clear contradiction, it will add money to their own and their employers' pockets. Since many of the most important decisions involved in the practice of medicine are judgmental, the temptation to base them on financial consequences, particularly in the absence of compelling clinical outcomes, is enormous and potentially detrimental to patients.

Further exacerbating this problem is the general decrease in physician compensation levels due to the increased market power of physician service buyers. This power is exercised in the form of capitated rates, which are set in a way that lowers physician income. As these forces impact physicians' bank accounts, they are trying to counter them and maintain their income levels by one of two strategies.

First, to counter shrinking fees for service, they are trying to run harder by providing more services per hour. As they try to squeeze in more patients and procedures, they shrink the time available to spend with each patient. The impact this has on quality is currently subject to much debate. As market forces continue to reduce fees, however, at some point physicians will find they cannot lose money on every encounter and make it up through volume.

The second strategy involves switching gears and trying to provide less service per patient on a capitated basis. This is a very appealing alternative to running harder because it states that *the less you do, the more you make.*

As the financial pressure mounts from these capitated systems, the economic incentives could potentially overwhelm the moral, ethical, and legal duties to care for patients. While it is assumed that the threat of malpractice will induce physicians to continue to care for their patients properly, this threat is an extremely poor substitute for well-thought-out compensation practices and quality control.

What the corporate world tells us

It is clear from years of research into compensation systems for corporate executives that if people are told to do A for the good of the company but are compensated to do B, they will consistently do B. For example, if an insurance executive is paid solely for revenue growth, he or she may work to grow revenue at the expense of profitability (e.g., by cutting prices).

The executive might do this despite the fact he or she is "told" to sell only profitable products. This is particularly disconcerting when applied to physician compensation. If the moral, ethical, and legal imperatives for a physician are to do A, but his or her compensation structure emphasizes B, then executive compensation research indicates the physician will do B. If B is undesirable for patients, there will be a conflict.

This is a critical issue that has significant implications for the delivery of medical care in the United States. To solve the problem, an entirely new reward architecture must be created to attract and motivate these highly educated, traditionally entrepreneurial employees. But it is equally critical that a new program must conform to a myriad of laws and also reflect the new challenges of a shifting paradigm.

As managed care companies increasingly offer low price, organizations that succeed in crafting well-designed compensation plans will be able to motivate the right behaviors and balance the competing interests of resource allocation and proper medical care. It is also clear that organizations taking the time and effort to get their compensation systems right are going to have vastly superior returns on their investment in physician acquisitions. By the same token, improvements in quality patient satisfaction will remain elusive when incentives are misaligned. Only by measuring and paying on these conflicting elements can a win–win situation be created for employers, patients, and physicians.

chapter eight

Disability: The Hidden Health Care Dilemma*

*It occurred to me that there was no difference between men, in intelligence or race, so profound as the difference between the sick and the well. ***

As the United States evolves toward a knowledge-based economy, the emphasis on maintaining a competitive workforce is moving toward center stage. When employees go out on disability, it is not just a matter of adding up the medical benefits bill and the income replacement costs; knowledge and experience are lost as well. Workplace efficiency — and often customer relationships — suffer in both the short and long run.

Organizations that do not manage disability programs risk lower productivity, a decline in competitiveness and a hit to the bottom line. The growing concern employers face is that both the direct and indirect costs associated with lost work time due to illness and injury will only continue to grow. According to calculations based on Census Bureau data, by the year 2000 total disability costs will top $340 billion — double what they were at the start of the decade.

To better document this trend, Watson Wyatt and the Washington Business Group on Health (WBGH) have surveyed employers related to disability management for the last three years. In 1998, the survey found that the costs of disability programs constituted

---

* This chapter is based on Watson Wyatt's 1996, 1997 and 1998/99 Staying @Work Integrated Disability Management survey reports produced jointly with the Washington Business Group on Health (WBGH).
** *The Great Gatsby*, F. Scott Fizgerald, Reprint edition, June 1996, C. Scribner Sons, New York, 1925.

a significant, yet little publicized, impact on payroll costs. Total direct disability costs as a percentage of payroll in the 1998 survey were 6.1 percent. Direct costs, however, tell only part of the story. The bill for indirect costs such as the cost of temporary workers, overtime, and the increased expense to benefit programs such as health care, pensions, and life insurance, add an additional 6.7 percent of payroll expense, raising the total bill to 12.8 percent (Figure 8.1).

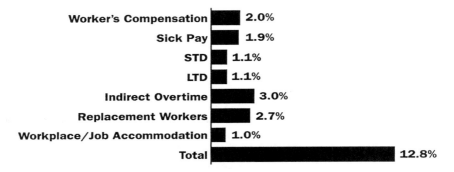

Figure 8.1   Average disability costs as a percentage of payroll. (Source: 1998/99 Staying @ Work, Third Annual Survey, Watson Wyatt Worldwide/WGBH.)

    To further inflate the price tag, other indirect costs that are more difficult to measure, yet very real, continue to grow. Examples of these indirect costs include unhappy customers who must wait longer than normal for goods or services, disgruntled coworkers who resent having to do the work of someone who is out on disability, and the associated costs of additional administration and claims processing. To make matters even worse, temporary replacement workers have less on-the-job experience, which could result in even more workplace injuries and displacements. To put it simply, the total health costs of disability-related illness and injury are high and going higher while organizational productivity and profits suffer.

What factors contribute to disability costs?

A combination of demographic, environmental, and benefit plan features are all responsible for the growth in disability costs and lost productive time. Demographic factors include an employee's age, primary occupation, and length of employment. The older an employee is, the more pronounced the impact of an illness or injury is likely to be and the higher the health care costs. In fact, more than one half of the respondents to the Watson Wyatt/WBGH 1998/99 disability survey said that age contributes to time lost from work, up from just 19 percent in 1996. As the baby boom generation grows older, the average age of the overall workforce is rising, so employers will face higher disability costs due to the aging factor alone. Income replacement costs incurred by disability-related absenteeism also will be higher because baby boomers account for the bulk of the workforce and typically earn more due to their longer job tenures.

Environmental factors such as the general work climate and management style will also impact costs. Corporate mergers, downsizings and/or restructurings help raise the general level of anxiety and stress, and perhaps fear of job loss. This can trigger an episode of disability. Also, for employees on disability, a changing work environment may cause them not to hurry to return to work if they think the position to which they would return has been restructured or even downsized, further raising the probability of even more job-related stress.

Even the design of a disability program can play an important role in determining the amount of lost work time. Well-designed plans provide incentives for an employee to return to work quickly, perhaps by providing an alternative work arrangement such as a modified duty program. On the other hand, plans without proper management could end up causing employees to stay out longer on disability, penalizing both them and their employers.

In addition, a managed health care program can often work at cross-purposes with a disability plan. Say, for example, that an employee is disabled with back injury and has two treatment options: bed rest under Option 1 or aggressive physical therapy under Option 2. Option 1 costs less under the medical plan and may be the treatment of choice for the managed care plan. Option 2 may have higher health care treatment costs, but it gets the employee back to work much sooner resulting in lower overall direct (medical) and indirect (replacement) costs, the employer's choice. How to best determine the optimal outcome for all three parties — the employer, employee and provider — is at the heart of the problem. Who is in charge? Who and what receive priority — the employee (patient), the provider (supplier) or the employer (payer)?

This growing list of factors points to the need for an integrated approach to disability management. Only an approach that can address the concerns of all the parties involved and coordinates all employer-sponsored health (managed care, carve-outs), employment (performance management, compensation, and training) and work or family policies and programs can have a lasting effect on total disability costs.

Integrated disability management

The concept of integrated disability management is a simple one: Connect all the individual care components so they complement each other. Integrated disability management coordinates occupational and non-occupational disability and other related programs — such as the group health plan, health promotion programs, and employee assistance programs (EAPs) — to bring down total costs, improve overall workforce health, and ease administration burdens. Such integration encompasses illness- and injury-prevention efforts, rehabilitation, medical case management, and return-to-work programs for all causes of disability.

Integration becomes complex, however, when considering the vast scope of the programs and behaviors to be integrated, ranging from front-line supervisor training supporting return-to-work, to the education of health care providers about the workplace, to the coordination of all medical and disability vendors. Every organization's situation is different; no single model of integration will work well for every company across the board. Further, integration exists as a continuum; some firms demonstrate a deep and energetic commitment to aligning every possible aspect, while others build upon a less comprehensive approach, integrating only one or two programs. Based on the 1998/99 disability survey, 42 percent of employers indicated they have integrated their programs while an additional 20 percent said they are planning to integrate. Among larger companies, the percentage is nearly double that of smaller companies, hopefully setting the pace for the entire marketplace and foretelling the coming trends.

The reward of integration

Why should employers integrate their plans? For one thing, the savings are significant. On average, surveyed employers reported that integrated disability management lowered their disability bill by 19 percent. But cost savings are not the only benefit. Despite measurement difficulties, respondents who have integrated the management of their disability programs reported improvements in productivity, customer satisfaction, and employee absenteeism (Figure 8.2).

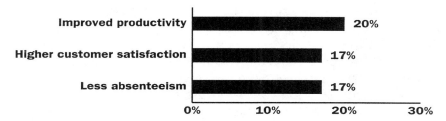

Figure 8.2   Has your integrated disability management program led to … (Source: 1998/99 Staying @ Work Third Annual Survey, Watson Wyatt World-wide/WBGH.)

Employers also rely on other surrogate measures besides cost savings to evaluate the effectiveness of their integrated disability programs. The most important of these measures are employee return-to-work rates and the duration of employee absence. Well over one-third of employers also are using employees' health status — the most important step prior to returning to work — as a measure to track the success of their integration efforts.

Learning from and leveraging past experience

The vast majority of employers have been diligent in managing their occupational disability programs, but most employers admit they do not manage their non-occupational programs as vigorously. However, a day lost is a day lost, regardless of the circumstances surrounding the disabling condition. An integrated program can apply many of the lessons learned in the administration of occupational disabilities to injuries and illnesses occurring off the job, helping to offset and reduce these costs as well.

Our ongoing surveys of disability programs show that, on both the occupational and the non-occupational side, the yardstick by which success is measured can make a difference in costs. The key is to focus on employee productivity. Companies that try to relate their integrated efforts to productivity improvement end up with greater cost reductions and lower overall costs, especially in their non-occupational programs.

The integration tool kit

Two of the most effective tools in conjunction with disability management are medical case management and modified duty programs. Case management protocols are simply predetermined guidelines for handling specific kinds of disabilities and illnesses. Their purpose is to prevent unnecessary treatments and ensure that proven treatment regimens are pursued consistently, so that affected individuals are returned to health as quickly as possible. Modified duty programs are designed to ease the transition back to work for an employee who has experienced either a temporary or permanent disabling condition. An example of such a program would be a warehouse worker with a knee injury being temporarily assigned to administrative functions. A more permanent workplace modification could be job-sharing or telecommuting to accommodate an employee who has incurred a lasting disability.

Benefits from these programs accrue to employer and employee alike. Employees sitting idly at home have negative productivity. They produce no output while generating high costs (both direct and indirect). This situation is not helpful to the company or to the employees. People need to feel a sense of purpose and accomplishment in their lives. Remaining off the job can contribute to a "disability mentality" and, in time, makes the employee's return to employment less likely.

For some employers, the assumed cost of necessary workplace modifications may be mitigating the rise of formal return-to-work programs. However, numerous studies have shown that such modifications are often either free or very inexpensive, especially when offset against the enormous costs of keeping someone at home.

Of course, an employer needs to avoid giving employees the impression that the only thing that matters is getting them back to work without also returning them to health. Our surveys show that organizations that place disproportionately more emphasis on return-to-work goals as opposed to returning employees to clinical health end up with higher costs and limited productivity improvements.

Incentives and accountability

To achieve true integration, everyone from line employees all the way through top management must cooperate. To promote commitment to the program, incentives like cash or other rewards for achieving desirable results for safety and injury prevention, as well as returning employees to work, may be justified, especially when it comes to non-occupational disability. Our survey found that effective firms place considerably more emphasis on safety and injury prevention than do less effective firms — which should prompt employers to consider offering incentives for both occupational and non-occupational programs.

Operational departments also should be held accountable for return-to-work results so that they will work to improve their claims experience. Employers who "charge back" disability costs to the originating department enforce accountability and focus on the link between lost time and productivity.

Integration: difficult but rewarding

Anything worth doing is usually difficult, and this is certainly the case with disability integration. Employers already have developed a number of effective tools and techniques to deal internally with occupational disability. Many, if not all, of these same tools have proven to be just as effective when used to address non-occupational disability.

The difficulty is that integrating many different programs poses significant challenges in coordinating among departments and obtaining the necessary benchmarking data. The most important step in overcoming these problems is to achieve early buy-in from top management for the integrated disability management effort. Only commitment from top management can ensure that all the disparate groups (human resources, risk, finance, compensation and benefits, systems, corporate communications, and the organization's operational divisions) will provide the necessary cooperation.

Other steps for successful integration include:

- Recognition that true integration is holistic; integrating only one or two aspects of the system will not yield the highest potential savings.
- All parties — supervisors, health care providers, employees, insurance carriers, and third-party administrators — must cooperate, and performance guarantees should be in place.
- Employees should be treated like the valuable human capital they are — capital that must be optimally engaged if the organization is to remain competitive.

- Employees should have ready access to high-quality, appropriate medical treatment and rehabilitative services for injuries sustained at work or off the job.

The future of integrated disability management

Historically, disability costs have appeared to be low in relation to other programs such as medical plan costs. But if employers look at the whole picture, direct and indirect costs of disability are larger than they seem and will increase substantially in the future, thanks to demographic and environmental trends. Organizations need to be prepared to address this issue effectively.

Moreover, integrated disability management will become essential for organizations that recognize the value of their human capital. Keeping workers healthy and productive — and, where necessary, returning them to work after a disability — is integral to a comprehensive disability management process. Such a process will be crucial to developing and retaining the workforce necessary to sustain an organization's competitive advantage.

chapter nine

Value Purchasing and Partnerships*

Nowadays people know the price of everything and the value of nothing.**

The health care purchasing decision has become increasingly complex and problematic.

Resurgent health care inflation, growing HMO profit pressures and health care industry turmoil have caused some managed care plans to submit premium increases in the double digits. The buyer's market of the mid-1990s is fast becoming a fading memory.

What can a purchaser or employer do? Buying on cost is seductively simple — a matter of finding the lowest-cost provider on the "spot market" for health care. But this approach can hurt quality or even result in fiduciary concerns. Alternatively, employers can take the more sophisticated route of balancing quality, access, and plan administration against the cost of the plan to maximize overall plan value.

To attain that value, employers must be proactive by developing a strategic plan and having a partner. Employers need to have a plan that makes the connection between the health care they purchase and the productivity of their workforce, and ultimately between their health care purchasing practices and shareholder value. Employers need a partnership that provides a stable framework. Stability allows both the employer and the health care pro-

---

* This chapter is based on Watson Wyatt's 1996, 1997, 1998 and 1999 surveys and reports on Purchasing Value in Health Care produced jointly with the Washington Business Group on Health (WBGH). Data also is included from Watson Wyatt's 1999 survey on providing value in health care produced jointly with the Healthcare Financial Management Association (HFMA).
** Oscar Wilde, in *The Picture of Dorian Gray.*

vider to invest in improving the quality of health care delivery without losing control of costs.

The price of quality

Over the past four years, employers responding to the Watson Wyatt/WBGH annual survey of value purchasing have stated that cost pressures have grown steadily and hurt the quality of care. Small employers are the most worried. Over half expressed concern in 1999, up from 33 percent in 1996.

Quality suffers when an employer's cost-driven focus results in switching providers, cost-shifting to employees or constantly changing plan benefits and/or coverage. Such short-term initiatives only disrupt the doctor–patient relationship and affect employee morale and satisfaction, while increasing the administrative burden on providers.

Health care providers also are concerned about cost pressures. More than half the participants in the 1999 survey stated that such pressures adversely affect the quality of care. Also, more than one-third (35 percent) of managed care organizations agreed that quality is suffering from cost pressures, up from just one out of five such organizations in 1996.

The cost of care

Health care inflation has been suppressed in the last few years as providers have kept premiums low in a fight for market share. Employers also have become smarter and more assertive in their health care purchasing. However, health care inflation is set to escalate again in 1999 as several market changes take hold:

- Providers turn their attention to revenue growth and maintaining profit margins.
- New lifestyle pharmaceuticals and expensive biomedical techniques become available.
- An aging population puts increasing demands on the medical system.

In fact, health care inflation may even exceed the projections of the survey's predicted increases for the second straight year (see Table 9.1).

Table 9.1 Employer Predictions of Future Health Care Premium Increases Over the Next Two to Three Years

Year	Small Employers	Medium Employers	Large Employers
1999	9.0%	8.1%	7.4%
1998	8.8%	7.3%	5.8%

Source: 1999 Fourth Annual Survey on Purchasing Value in Health Care, Watson Wyatt/WBGH

The race for revenue and market share has led to consolidation and rapid change in the health care industry. Survey respondents indicated such changes would continue to affect numerous aspects of their health care plans and the quality of care their employees receive. Cost competitiveness may have helped to hold down costs, but concerns about access and administrative issues continue. Moreover, the move toward for-profit providers has only seemed to exacerbate these concerns (Table 9.2).

Table 9.2 Effect of Rapid Change on Health Care Plans

All Firms	Improved	Worsened
Cost competitiveness	64%	13%
Quality	21%	25%
Access	30%	34%
Administration	46%	44%
How has the growth in for-profit health care providers affected quality of care?	13%	39%

Source: 1999 Fourth Annual Survey on Purchasing Value in Health Care, Watson Wyatt/WBGH

So how will employers and providers react if and when their own premiums — or costs of delivering health care — go up? A large number of employers and providers are prepared to fall back on cost-shifting and renegotiating fees with each other. Employers also think they can simply change the benefits offered, while providers will try to cut the services they offer.

Purchased properly, health care contributes to the productivity and well being of a modern organization's most prized resources — its people. But to move toward value, companies need more than short-term solutions based on reductions in cost- and benefits. Employers and providers alike need a strategic plan and a partner.

Health care and strategic planning

Employers recognize the importance of health care benefits for attraction, retention, and workforce productivity. A plan for linking health care expenditures to human capital goals and shareholder value is critical to ensure that health care will be part of a company's strategic planning, not a perennial target for corporate budget-cutters.

The initial stage in forming such a plan is for employers to define what they think constitutes value in a health plan. According to our survey, employers are looking not only at cost, but also at the quality of care and employee satisfaction (Figure 9.1).

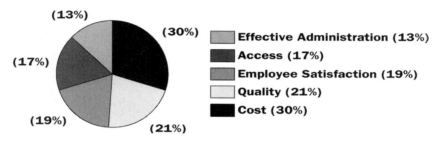

Figure 9.1   How would you weigh the above factors in purchasing health care? *Source*: 1999 Fourth Annual Survey on Purchasing Value in Health Care, Watson Wyatt/WBGH

Having identified what they believe constitutes a high-quality health plan, over half of the surveyed employers are trying to educate their employees about plan options and how to use them effectively. Financial and other incentives also are being used to encourage employees to select plans identified as having higher quality, lower costs, and better administration. The more commonplace incentives include lower employee expenditures and more-comprehensive coverage (Table 9.3).

Table 9.3   Incentives to Affect Employee Health Plan Choice

	Small Employers	Medium Employers	Large Employers	Total
Lower employee contribution	69%	72%	70%	71%
Lower co-pays	59%	62%	47%	58%
Lower deductibles	52%	57%	30%	50%
Additional coverage	28%	34%	20%	30%

Source: 1999 Fourth Annual Survey on Purchasing Value in Health Care, Watson Wyatt/WB-GH

Some employers are taking an even more active role in the provision of health care. Nearly one-quarter (23 percent) are engaged in direct contracting for the delivery of health care services, while another 17 percent have embarked on specific multiyear health and productivity improvement initiatives with their providers.

Defining health care quality

Setting performance and quality measures against which a health plan can be evaluated is now becoming a part of nearly all employers' health planning, from readily observable information like cost and access, to quality-based measures like (Health Plan Employer Data Information Set [HEDIS]) and accreditation status. As in previous years, large employers with more resources are more likely to use more-sophisticated evaluation measures. Nevertheless, smaller employers are using these measures more than ever before (Table 9.4).

Table 9.4 Do You Use the Following Measures to Evaluate
Health Care Plans?

		Small Firms	Large Firms
Accreditation Status[1]	1999	31%	67%
	1996	17%	60%
Quality Improvement Initiatives	1999	21%	53%
	1996	28%	55%
HEDIS	1999	16%	63%
	1996	5%	54%

[1] In 1996, accreditation status was "NCQA accreditation status."

Source: 1996 and 1999 Surveys on Purchasing Value in Health Care, Watson Wyatt/WBGH

It is not sufficient to have a good plan, however. An employer needs a partner to help carry out the plan.

The partnership advantage

The need to establish longer-term continuity to adequately address employer-specific health needs has led to the growth of partnerships between employers and providers.

More than one-third (35 percent) of the employers surveyed say they have established a long-term partnership with a health care provider. Large employers (53 percent) were almost twice as likely as small organizations (32 percent) to enter into such arrangements. Fewer health care providers (27 percent) seem to consider themselves in a partnership arrangement, although 40 percent of managed care organizations say they currently partner with employers.

How does a partnership work?

Partnership is generally defined as a multi-year arrangement where both parties share an ongoing commitment to a multi-year timeframe without the annual switching of providers or networks.

Each year over the course of the partnership, Watson Wyatt encourages providers to commit to a 5 percent improvement in medical outcomes and a 5 percent drop in administrative overhead.

How is that possible? A partnership frees the provider from annual marketing and enrollment-related expenses. The provider also gains a guaranteed base of patients and is thus motivated to invest in improving the efficiency of health care delivery through focused preventive, targeting, and wellness efforts.

A partnership also rewards employers and their employees with consistent, value-based health care coverage, without the disruptions caused by frequent switching of providers. To make a partnership work, however, employers need to proactively manage the relationship. Employers must collect relevant data on plan usage, medical utilization and the like. They also need to conduct regular, comprehensive audits of the plan's clinical, technological, and administrative performance to ensure that the provider continues to meet the objectives set forth in the partnership agreement.

Partnership rewards

Large employers that partnered were more likely to report lower expected annual premium increases — 6 percent versus 7.5 percent annual increases for all other employers. In addition, employers that partnered were more confident — and more assertive — purchasers of health care. They were also more apt to see a connection between health care spending, quality, performance, and employee health and productivity (Table 9.5).

Employers and providers: are they on the same page?

Despite the importance and success of partnering, employers and providers still see their working relationship differently. Providers are much more likely to characterize the relationship with employ-

Table 9.5 The Partnership Advantage

Employers who:	Partner	Don't Partner
Say they are "very effective" at getting value for their health care dollar	9%	5%
Are interested in direct contracting with providers	40%	13%
Use employer-specified performance goals	52%	41%
Have long-term strategy to integrate health care and disability programs	43%	32%
Say health care benefits are "very important" in increasing productivity	29%	20%
Have regular, scheduled communication with provider to discuss performance	80%	49%
Try to determine the impact of health plans on productivity	25%	14%

Source: 1999 Fourth Annual Survey on Purchasing Value in Health Care, Watson Wyatt/WBGH

ers as adversarial. They also are far less likely than an employer to describe the relationship as a partnership (Table 9.6).

Table 9.6 How Would You Describe Your Current Relationship with Your Health Care Plan Provider (Purchaser-Employer)?

	Adversarial/ Uneasy Truce	Business/ Supplier	Partners
What employers say above providers	22%	56%	18%
What providers say about employers	36%	54%	4%

Source: 1999 Fourth Annual Survey on Purchasing Value in Health Care, Watson Wyatt/WBGH and the 1999 Second Annual Survey on Providing Value in Health Care, Watson Wyatt/HFMA

Employers and providers also do not see eye to eye when it comes to purchasing health care effectively. More than half of the providers surveyed (54 percent) say employers are either "not very effective" or "not effective at all" in getting value for their dollar.

Value purchasing

Even in the face of growing cost pressures, a significant number of both employers (35 percent) and providers (51 percent) still think they can purchase or supply the same quality of health care at the same or lower costs. Employers and providers generally agree that improvements in the way care is managed and the use of technology hold the most promise for true quality gains (Table 9.8). Providers also say there is still excess capacity in the health care system to be "wrung out," while employers point to market pressure on providers to maintain quality and cost competitiveness. Though these may be viable short-term solutions, it is important for employers to think longer term — develop a plan and form a partnership to maximize overall plan value.

Table 9.6   How Health Care Quality Can Be Maintained Next Year
at the Same Or Lower Costs

	Employers	Providers
Still excess capacity in the health care system	29%	40%
More effective technology for administration	43%	55%
Direct negotiation	39%	17%
Improvements in the way care is managed	58%	81%
Market pressure on providers	48%	22%

Source: 1999 Fourth Annual Survey on Purchasing Value in Health Care, Watson Wyatt/WB-GH and the 1999 Second Annual Survey on Provinding Value in Health Care, Watson Wyatt/HFMA.

Purchasing health care will continue to be difficult, with costs going up and the provider market in flux. The temptation to focus solely on cost is strong. But such a focus can lead only to lower quality in the short term, and higher costs in the long term. The key is to purchase value. Developing strategic plans to improve the connection among health care, productivity, and shareholder value is the first step. Forming partnerships with providers to improve quality and accountability is the second. In response, the provider community will have to improve the delivery of care to meet the needs of a more sophisticated and demanding customer base.

Conclusion

I have attempted to describe some of the challenges and opportunities that will be bearing down on us with regard to providing health care in the U.S. and around the world. Clearly, over the next several decades, an aging population will have a great impact on the demand for health care around the world. The number of people over age 85 is expected to grow from 3 million today to 20 million in the U.S. by 2020. Unless medical knowledge advances, almost half of that population, or nearly 10 million Americans, can expect to be suffering from some form of dementia. The stress and strain on the health care system to provide the needed care for this group alone will be enormous. Further, medical science continues to convert acute, relatively inexpensive, life-ending illnesses into chronic, long-term and expensive conditions. These advances will impact the lives of tens of millions. As a result, the financial capacity to pay for this care will be stretched to the breaking point.

The current pay-as-you-go model, foisted on us by politicians, is an intellectually, morally, and financially bankrupt promise. The current health care delivery system, composed of isolated providers and controlled by managed care organizations whose systems resemble a chewing-gum-and-duct-tape arrangement, is simply inadequate to care for the coming needs of the population.

The real question confronting us as a society is whether we will have the will to embark on the difficult path of building a truly efficient health care delivery system as opposed to being seduced by the seemingly easier path offered by a hollow system. I believe we can harness scientific advances, information technology and our knowledge of preventive medicine to create a compassionate, efficient delivery system that is able to meet the needs of the population and bring the quality of life to new heights. In order to create this future, however, a tremendous amount of political will and courage will be needed to generate the reforms required to alter our trajectory.

If we are unable to muster that courage, then the path of least resistance will continue to lead us toward a Hollowcare model. Patient care will continue to deteriorate, with greater pressure on individuals to care for their families in a system totally inadequate for all but the wealthiest.

All the ingredients necessary to create an efficient, compassionate system exist today. But the longer we take to alter care, the more difficult it will become to fix. If meaningful change is to occur, we need to start today to engage in a national and global debate on what we want for our parents, our children and ourselves.

Index